"This accessible but penetrating book shows culture provides liturgies: soul-shaping pra us to turn from God to the sovereign self, fr created reality, from living for truth and love to living for power — , can't see them, you can't resist them, and the author gives you resources to do both. Samuel James has written an essential book. He is one of the small but growing number of young thinkers to whom the church must listen if it is to learn how to be effective in evangelism and formation in a post-Christendom world."

Tim Keller, Founding Pastor, Redeemer Presbyterian Church, New York City; Cofounder, Redeemer City to City

"This is such a wise and insightful book. Its power lies in the way it exposes truths not just about the digital world but about us: the things we want, the way we try to find them, how the internet weaponizes them in ways we may not have noticed, and what we can do about it. Penetrating without being frightening, and positive without being naïve, *Digital Liturgies* is the guide we need."

Andrew Wilson, Teaching Pastor, King's Church London

"*Digital Liturgies* is a book that issues both a challenge and a call. Samuel James challenges our perspective by pulling back the curtain so we see that technology's effects are not neutral, and our digital habits tilt us toward an online world that makes the wisdom of God seem like foolishness. But James also calls us to a better way, reorienting us toward greater understanding, wisdom, and the practices of resistance necessary for faithful and fruitful living. An accessible book full of profound insight."

Trevin Wax, Vice President of Research and Resource Development, The North American Mission Board; Visiting Professor, Cedarville University; author, *The Thrill of Orthodoxy*, *Rethink Your Self*, and *This Is Our Time*

"Virtually everyone I know feels exhausted by or enslaved to some aspect of digital life. In this book, one of the sharpest Christian minds helps us discover what exactly we're looking for in our screens. *Digital Liturgies* points a path beyond the outrage, anger, shame, and boredom that we accidentally download into our souls."

Russell Moore, Editor in Chief, *Christianity Today*

"After the first few chapters, I decided my teenagers should read this book, and maybe their whole school as well. Such good sociological insights. A few chapters later I decided I wanted my church to read it. Such helpful spiritual and pastoral insights too. By the book's end, however, I realized I needed this book. It applied the gospel to me and my online habits, and I need worthier ones. What that means, friend, is that I'm pretty sure you also need this book. It explains the digital water we're all swimming in and how that digital water has reprogrammed us more than we realize."

Jonathan Leeman, Editorial Director, 9Marks; Elder,
Cheverly Baptist Church, Hyattsville, Maryland

"Modern-day Christians are so trained to think about the *what* (content) that we don't often enough consider the *how* (form). *Digital Liturgies*—wisely, clearly, and compellingly—helps us to consider the ways in which we are formed by the digital world in which we live. Samuel James not only introduces some of the most important thinkers on this most defining quality of our age, but he also offers his own fresh insights."

Karen Swallow Prior, author, *The Evangelical Imagination:
How Stories, Images, and Metaphors Created a Culture in Crisis*

"Secular man is trying to supplant the divine Creator with a false one—the almighty algorithm. As Samuel James argues, we utilize digital tools believing that through them, we can make the world into our own image. With careless passivity, digital tools end up conforming us into its Silicon Valley–engineered image—alienated, fragmented, compulsive, and angry. There is no evangelical thinker I am aware of who has thought as critically, cautiously, and self-critically about the toll of digital life on our spirituality, psychology, and embodiment as Samuel James. From one of the most talented writers of his generation of evangelical thinkers, *Digital Liturgies* is one of the smartest books I've read from one of evangelicalism's brightest lights."

Andrew T. Walker, Associate Professor of Christian Ethics,
The Southern Baptist Theological Seminary; Fellow,
The Ethics and Public Policy Center

Digital Liturgies

Digital Liturgies

Rediscovering Christian Wisdom in an Online Age

Samuel D. James

WHEATON, ILLINOIS

Digital Liturgies: Rediscovering Christian Wisdom in an Online Age

© 2023, 2025 by Samuel D. James

Published by Crossway
      1300 Crescent Street
      Wheaton, Illinois 60187

Cover Design: Jordan Singer

First printing 2023

Reprinted with study questions 2025

Printed in the United States of America

Trade paperback ISBN: 978-1-4335-9919-4
ePub ISBN: 978-1-4335-9921-7
PDF ISBN: 978-1-4335-9920-0

Library of Congress Cataloging-in-Publication Data

Names: James, Samuel, 1988– author.

Title: Digital liturgies : rediscovering Christian wisdom in an online age / Samuel D. James.

Description: Wheaton, Illinois : Crossway, 2023. | Includes bibliographical references and index.

Identifiers: LCCN 2022050804 (print) | LCCN 2022050805 (ebook) | ISBN 9781433587139 (trade paperback) | ISBN 9781433587146 (pdf) | ISBN 9781433587160 (epub)

Subjects: LCSH: Technology—Religious aspects—Christianity. | Social media—Religious aspects—Christianity.

Classification: LCC BR115.T42 J36 2023 (print) | LCC BR115.T42 (ebook) | DDC 261.5/6—dc23/eng/20230512

LC record available at https://lccn.loc.gov/2022050804

LC ebook record available at https://lccn.loc.gov/2022050805

Crossway is a publishing ministry of Good News Publishers.

VP		35	34	33	32	31	30	29	28	27	26	25
13	12	11	10	9	8	7	6	5	4	3	2	1

For
Mom and Dad

Contents

Introduction

What the Web Means for Our Spiritual Lives

I REGISTERED FOR my first Facebook account the summer after graduating high school. Like so many others, I started using the site because friends were already there, and the last thing you want to do in high school is miss what everyone else is doing. I signed up, quickly sent friend requests to Andrew and a couple other guys in my class, and assumed this quaint little thing would add up to a few hours of social fun and maybe a way to keep in touch with some classmates who were going out of state to college.

In other words, I wasn't at all prepared for the spell that Facebook would work on me.

The hook was almost instant. It only took a couple weeks before I was compulsively checking Facebook as often as possible to see if anyone had responded to my friend requests (or even better, if someone had sent one to me!). Even after adding only a few dozen friends, looking through profiles (we used to jokingly call it "stalking") started to take up bigger and bigger chunks of my day. In the early days before the "Like" button, if you wanted people to know you appreciated their profile picture or a funny status, you had to comment on it. Notifications for comments became a deliriously intense source of both satisfaction and anxiety. Somehow, an entire adolescence's worth of insecurity, crushes, ambition, and identity became compressed and contained inside a small, red, pixelated square at the upper corner of our family PC.

A story like that probably hits close to home for many, and if that were all there is to it, it might be little more than a warmly nostalgic remembrance of a piece of pop culture that we all seemed to share for a few years during the Barack Obama administration. But that's not all there is to it.

Like many others, my story doesn't end with a few nondescript years of Facebook use, followed by an adulthood that left algorithms behind. Rather, my first Facebook account in the summer of 2007 was the beginning of a way of living that was completely foreign to my parents. As the years passed, Facebook changed designs and features, but what didn't change was how central digital media had become to my normal life. Instead of being a diversion that I stowed away in the corner for occasional use during the doldrums of offline life, my online activity became the most consistent, the most regular, the most habitual thing about me.

I would go to classes, then scroll Facebook. A couple hours at church on Sunday were followed by several hours of email, instant messenger, and (later) YouTube. Through the years, the centrality of the social internet was established more and more for me personally as well as seemingly everyone else. Blogs and tweets took up a huge percentage of my reading; I became twice as likely to text someone than call, even family. The transformation in the broader society became evident as I got older, as almost everyone I knew began talking about "fasting" from social media or their New Year's resolutions to look less frequently at screens.

In just a few years, these digital technologies had gone from something we were all excited to try, to something we were all desperate to somehow escape (at least temporarily).

That's one story, which a lot of us now in our mid-thirties know well. But there's another story to tell about our relationship to digital technology, and it's about much more than how much time we burn on it. This story is about the way that these technologies shape and mold. It's about what it means to be humans, created in God's image, whose lives are increasingly mediated by screens, algorithms, and pixels. What if the reality we need to face is not so much about how we overuse and overlove a valuable tool, but about what happens when a tool is no longer just a tool? What if the issue is not that we aren't making the internet more humane; it's that the internet is making us less so?

What's Water?

In 2005 Kenyon College invited the writer David Foster Wallace to deliver the commencement address. Wallace began his speech to the graduating class with a short fable. Two young fish are swimming in the ocean, and eventually an older fish greets them. "Hello, boys. How's the water?" The two young fish look at each other completely confused, and then ask: "What is water?"

"The point of the fish story," Wallace explained, "is merely that the most obvious, important realities are often the ones that are hardest to see and talk about." This illustration, while also good for a light chuckle from an audience, communicates a profound truth. What we are immersed in is taken for granted, and what is taken for granted is not thought about. Wallace wanted the graduating class of Kenyon College to know that the hardest task that awaited

3

them was not "changing the world" or "making a difference," but paying attention to the right things:

> Twenty years after my own graduation, I have come gradually to understand that the liberal arts cliché about teaching you how to think is actually shorthand for a much deeper, more serious idea: learning how to think really means learning how to exercise some control over how and what you think. It means being conscious and aware enough to choose what you pay attention to and to choose how you construct meaning from experience. Because if you cannot exercise this kind of choice in adult life, you will be totally hosed.[1]

In other words, we are the fish. We swim each day in the depths of our modern world, floating past places, things, and ideas that we don't even see because of how familiar they are. We take our day-in, day-out life utterly for granted, not consciously but automatically, and the result is that we rarely if ever think seriously about those things that are closest to our experiences. We just accept them without trying, like a fish spends a lifetime without ever knowing that the world he lives in is called "water."

Being unable to notice or think reflectively about something does not change its reality. Taking something for granted does not diminish its significance any more than living in an underground shelter darkens the sun. What Wallace was getting at in his speech to the graduates of Kenyon College was that our ability or inability to really see the "water" of reality around us is ultimately about how well *we* are living. The water is there; it's a given, inescapable.

1 David Foster Wallace, "This Is Water," commencement speech (2005), *fs* blog, accessed November 14, 2022, https://fs.blog/.

The question is not whether we will live in the water; the question is whether we will be able to see it as water.

This Is Water

Because the social internet has come to dominate and reorient our lives, it can be difficult to imagine how it might be affecting our emotions, our values, or our worldview.[2] Many people who are young enough to feel invested in social media are not old enough to clearly remember life before it, while often those who can remember life before social media simply have no category for the immersive effect that it has on those who are younger. Further, the sheer omnipresence of digital technology can obscure its nature. As the social internet seems to blend in seamlessly to the fabric of day-in, day-out life, it doesn't occur to us that it could actually be bringing an ideology or a value system into our lives. Like fish in water, it's just all we know, so we don't see it clearly.

Over the past several years, Christian theologians and others have described the emerging generation of Western adults as belonging to the spirit of "expressive individualism." The scholar Robert Bellah defines expressive individualism this way: "Expressive individualism holds that each person has a unique core of feeling and intuition that should unfold or be expressed if individuality is to be realized."[3] In other words, what most people in the modern, secular world believe is that the key to their happiness, fulfillment, and quest for meaning in life is to arrange things so that their inner desires and ambitions can be totally achieved. If these desires and ambitions

---

2   I first heard the term *social internet* from my friend Chris Martin. See his book *Terms of Service: The Real Cost of Social Media* (Nashville, TN: B&H, 2022).

3   Robert Bellah, cited in Carl Trueman, "How Expressive Individualism Threatens Civil Society," Heritage Foundation, May 27, 2021, https://www.heritage.org/.

align with those of the community or the religion, great! But if not, then it's the community or the religion that must be changed or done away with. Life's center of gravity, according to expressive individualism, is the self.

In his helpful book *Rethink Yourself*, Trevin Wax describes this worldview as the call to "look in," to peer inside your own wants and sense of self to find meaning in life. He writes:

> The "look in" approach to life means that your purpose is to look inside yourself in order to discover who you truly are—to find what makes you unique—and then to take hold of your authentic self and emerge with it intact and uncompromised. Who are you? Only you can figure out the answer, and the way you find out is by looking deep into your heart to discover your uniqueness, to come to terms with what you most want from life.[4]

Expressive individualism is the quintessential secular creed. It is the chorus of nearly every chart-topping song, the subtext of every Disney film, the final resting place of contemporary education, parenting, and even much contemporary religion. How and why this happened is a fascinating story.[5] For now, the point to take away is that expressive individualism is part of the "water" that surrounds us modern, twenty-first-century people. We rarely notice it because it is all we know, yet we remain immersed.

4 Trevin Wax, *Rethink Yourself: The Power of Looking Up Before Looking In* (Nashville, TN: B&H, 2020), 11.

5 See Carl Trueman, *The Rise and Triumph of the Modern Self: Cultural Amnesia, Expressive Individualism, and the Road to Sexual Revolution* (Wheaton, IL: Crossway, 2020); Charles Taylor, *A Secular Age* (Cambridge, MA: Harvard University Press, 2007); Yuval Levin, *The Fractured Republic: Renewing America's Social Contract in the Age of Individualism* (New York: Basic, 2017).

What's crucial to realize is that alongside the philosophical revolution of expressive individualism, the digital technology revolution has exploded, and in the process it has provided the revolution of expressive individualism with its most important, most enchanting, and most effective vehicle.

What you and I know as the internet is a very recent development; the barest, most essential version of internet computing existed in the latter half of the twentieth century, but it was unusable for anyone except trained professionals. The commercial internet—otherwise known as the World Wide Web—is a product of the 1990s. In 1997 about 21 percent of Americans said they had used an internet technology in the past three months. In 2007 that percentage was 75 percent. By 2018 over 85 percent of Americans—or about 250 million people—were using internet technology at least semiregularly.[6] Perhaps even more significantly, the number of people who spend much of their time logged on has skyrocketed in recent years: 85 percent of US adults report being online every day, and about a third say they are online "almost constantly."[7] In other words, in about twenty years the internet has gone from a hobby of the few to the routine of the majority.

Part of the reason for this is that the internet has not just stayed a recreational pastime, a way to watch funny videos, read sports statistics, or send the occasional email. Many industries are now centered around the internet. These jobs require constant access to email, videoconferencing, file hosting, social media, and more. In the twenty-first century, it is perfectly plausible that a typical

6   "Share of the Population Using the Internet," International Telecommunication Union, Our World in Data, accessed November 14, 2022, https://ourworldindata.org/.
7   Andrew Perrin and Sara Atske, "About Three-in-Ten US Adults Say They Are 'Almost Constantly' Online," Pew Research Center, March 26, 2021, https://www.pewresearch.org/.

employed person would spend most (if not all) of his workday online, spend most (if not all) of his break catching up on social media or listening to a podcast, and then go home to spend most (if not all) of his free time watching Netflix, playing online games, or just browsing the web.

While some of us can still feel occasional pangs of guilt for "bingeing" too much TV or losing track of time aimlessly scrolling through our social media feeds, the point is that this kind of rhythm does not stand out as strange in our modern world. We can tinker around the edges, but the life bordered on all sides by the internet is neither rare nor surprising in our era. From work to dating, from movies to music, from friendship to even church—the screen is mediating much of our modern life.

If the web is the water we live in, expressive individualism is the chlorine that permeates it.

Tool or Teacher?

The internet is a lot like pornography.

No, that's not a typo. I did not mean to say that the internet *contains* a lot of pornography. I mean to say that the internet itself—i.e., its very nature—is like pornography. There's something about it that is pornographic in its essence.

If this sounds confusing, you're not alone. It sounds confusing because over the past few decades, the tendency among Christians has been to focus on what the internet provides instead of what it is. Consequently, evangelicals have indeed talked a lot about the scourge of online pornography. But while much attention has been given to how the web can supply us with spiritually dangerous pictures and videos, much less attention has been given to how the *very form* of the web shapes us in the image of the spirit of the age.

Few Christians would dispute that there is much on the internet that harms us. But by divorcing what the internet presents from what the internet intrinsically is, we are fighting against the symptoms of a more fundamental disease that we are failing to treat. "Staying pure online" is a worthy ambition, but defining purity to mean only one thing—the avoidance of certain content—not only misses the richer biblical ideal of wise living, but it ironically makes us more vulnerable to the allure of godless ideas and rhythms of life. It is entirely possible—in fact, all variables equal, it is likely—to faithfully avoid vulgar or explicit content on the web while simultaneously being shaped by it in a profoundly sub-Christian way.

This may sound incredibly strange. If we are avoiding sinful content online, how in the world can the internet "shape" us in a negative way? We try to avoid articles, podcasts, or videos that undermine Christian belief. Technology is a neutral tool; what matters is how we use it, right? The key (many might say) is to use the web only for good things: to keep up with friends, to consume wholesome content, to be more efficient at our work and school. Resist the allure of pornography or anti-Christian content, and the web is our friend, right?

This book tries to explain why the assumptions in the above paragraph are not quite right. Rather than being a neutral tool, the internet (particularly the social internet) is an epistemological environment[8]—a spiritual and intellectual habitat—that creates in its members particular ways of thinking, feeling, and believing. It's true in one sense that the web *is* a tool that responds to its users' desires. But the web is not a tool in the same way that a screwdriver

8 Epistemology is the branch of philosophy that asks about knowledge: how we can know things, what it means to believe correctly, etc.

or wrench is a tool. The web *speaks* to us. We talk to the web, and the web talks back, and this dialogue constitutes an ever-growing aspect of life in the digital age.

Rather than thinking of the web and social media as merely neutral tools that merely do whatever users ask of them, it is better to think of them as kinds of spaces that are continually shaping us to think, feel, communicate, and live in certain ways. In other words, the social internet is a liturgical environment. James K. A. Smith has written powerfully about the effect that certain habits and environments can have on our desires.[9] As we will see later on, even our most allegedly "nonreligious" spaces are deeply spiritual. They tell us a story about the good life: what it is, and how we can get it. These spiritual habitats train our hearts and make certain ideas and behaviors more desirable, and others less so, by immersing us in a particular narrative.

The web tells a story too. The disembodied, fragmented nature of the internet is not merely a quirk but a fundamental part of the web's nature and, thus, part of the story it tells. As we will see, the form of the internet has radically altered how we read, think, feel, and believe. The digital liturgies of the web and social media train us to invest ultimate authority in our own stories and experiences as they separate us from the objective givenness of the embodied world. How is it that in a supposedly relativistic, you-do-you age, so many people have been shamed or "dragged" online, helplessly watching their reputation or career be destroyed? The answer is not just that some people are mean but that the *form* of the web undermines moral reconciliation.

9   James K. A. Smith, *Desiring the Kingdom: Worship, Worldview, and Cultural Formation* (Grand Rapids, MI: Baker Academic, 2009), 19–27.

These are some of the "digital liturgies" that you and I encounter almost every day. They are not neutral. They are theological, philosophical, existential, and moral stories that leave constant impressions on us. They are soul-shaping narratives.

The Gospel's Analog Truth

One of the great things about being a Christian is that in a listless and frantic age, you don't have to chase after every new idea or attitude. To be a Christian is to go to bed every night knowing that you have a completely trustworthy, completely solid, and completely good word from the Creator of the universe. The maker of the stars put the wisdom, truth, and hope we need in a book, the Bible. The Bible reveals to us the grand narrative, the master story, that gives meaning and direction to our lives: the gospel of Jesus.

David Foster Wallace said his hope for the graduating class of Kenyon College was that by beginning to see reality for what it is, they would be able to "construct meaning from experience." The challenge for Christians in the digital age is different. We don't have to construct meaning; we have to cling to the meaning we've been given already.

Amid the white noise of digital liturgies that preach to us every day, the gospel is wonderfully satisfying analog truth. We'll say more about this later, but for now, by "analog truth" I mean that the story of the gospel is rooted deeply in physical reality. To preserve the good news of Jesus, God put his gospel in a physical book, inspiring real humans by the Holy Spirit to write physical words that tell a unified story about a speaking God, who was incarnated as a real human being to save us from our sin, free us from the slavery of self-obsession, and one day raise us up, body *and* soul, to live forever with him.

When we put the digital liturgies of our age up against the analog truth of the gospel, we see just how flimsy, how untrue, and how unsatisfying the spirit of the web age really is.

Before we begin, I want to offer one definition and two disclaimers.

First, in this book I will be using words like *internet*, *web*, *social media*, and *digital technology*. In most cases, these words will be used to refer to the same thing. This is important to acknowledge at the outset because, in technical terms, the internet, the web, social media, and digital technology are all distinct items. They share several things in common but are not the same thing. Throughout this book, however, these words will refer to one single idea: *the disembodied electronic environment that we enter through connected devices for the purpose of accessing information, relationships, and media that are not available to us in a physical format.*

Next, the first disclaimer: this book will not argue that Christians should stay off the internet. I'm not going to tell you to permanently unplug, find a cabin in the wilderness, and go "off the grid" so that you can be a better Christian. Not only would this be undoable for most of the people reading this; it would not accomplish what we might want it to. When Jesus prayed for his disciples a few hours before being crucified, he specifically prayed that instead of being taken out of the world, his followers would be preserved by the power of God's truth (John 17:15–17). Our immersion in the world's liturgies is not the deciding factor in our faithfulness to or love of Jesus. Rather, by identifying how the web shapes us, we can use these technologies more deliberately, more wisely, and more Christianly. To be in the world is not necessarily to be of the world.

Second, this book should not be read as a sermon by someone who has perfected what he is preaching. Something closer to the opposite is true: much of the last decade-plus of my life has been a struggle to reclaim my time, attention, and affection away from the ephemera of online existence. That struggle has probably seen more failures than victories. What follows is the result not of an exemplary lifestyle but of a journey to understand spiritual and mental tensions within myself and within others close to me.

The formative power of the web matters to me because I have experienced it in myself and in others. I have felt a change in the way I read and think that I believe is directly connected to how the web has dominated most of my adult life. I have noticed changes in myself and in people I know: not just personality tics but meaningful shifts in how we form our opinions, how we relate to those who disagree, and how we invest our time.

Many times over the last several years I have experienced a sense that the truths of Scripture feel foolish or implausible, not because of any strong argument I encountered against them, but simply because they felt out of step with the ideas and memes and mentalities that proliferate online. And especially in the past few years, I've seen and heard testimonies of genuine, God-fearing people who became deeply foolish—not because of intellectual deficiency, but by giving themselves over day after day to petty controversies, cheap outrage, and minute arguments. So many times, when these problems have emerged, a digital liturgy that took root in the heart has been the culprit.

This is the story for many of us. It's a story about technology, yes. But more deeply, it's a story about worship.

PART 1

TRUTH AND TECHNOLOGY

AS WE THINK ABOUT the formative power of online technology in our lives, we must start where all truth starts—with God. One of the reasons so few people can articulate the effects of the online world is that so few people have a baseline standard of human flourishing for comparison. The world is a thoroughly "tech-maximalist" place. As we will see, this is not an accident. Part of the reason is that much of our digital technology was invented according to a logic that sought to help humans transcend their humanness and achieve something more. Indeed, if there is truly nothing more to being human than endlessly optimizing ourselves, this makes perfect sense. Why not use every tool imaginable to escape the confines of our bodies?

Christianity, however, contradicts this narrative. As we open the Bible, God's word to all humanity, we see a meaning and a purpose much different. We see that we are not self-made but created in another's image. We see that we are not infinite or self-existent, but creatures who depend on the world around us and on each other. Most importantly, we see that the question of how we should live, rather than being an unknowable mystery or a self-chosen adventure, is a truth we must receive. There is an objectiveness to reality to which we as human creatures must conform if we are to live whole and well. The Bible calls our response to this objective reality "wisdom." Wisdom is real; wisdom is embodied. And it is wisdom that is obscured in a digital world.

What is this wisdom? What does it consist of? And how exactly does our digital technology challenge our pursuit of wisdom? Those are the topics of part 1. My hope is to convince you in these pages that Scripture offers all of us a way of living that is both gloriously transcendent and radically practical. It is a gospel liturgy that offers staggeringly more than the enticing escape of digital life.

1

Embodied Wisdom in a Faceless Age

IN THE BLACK RECESSES of lonely space, a well-dressed man arrives nearly silent on an enormous space station. Before he begins his important astronomical work, he goes to a wall in the station, where there is a screen about the size of a small television. Almost absentmindedly, the man punches a few keys near the screen. In a matter of seconds, a face appears, looking at him through the glass: his daughter, on earth. Her visage is as clear and bright as if she were standing in front of him rather than on her bed some 230,000 miles away. Across such a chasmic gap, they talk with one another in tones no louder than if they were only a few feet apart. The video call is live and crystal clear, the audio perfect and near-instant. After a brief conversation, they say their goodbyes, and the last act for both of them is to reach their arm somewhere just out of camera shot to switch an unseen button. The monitor goes blank, and they are, once again, planets apart.

Because you are reading this at some point (most likely!) in the twenty-first century, the scene I've just described sounds like it could be some overwrought description of a normal day for any astronaut in the Western world. Nothing about it feels extraordinary, because all of the technology in that paragraph, and the experience that the technology facilitated, is taken for granted in our era. We have names for it, like FaceTime, Skype, live-streaming, and 5G. Even those of us who prefer not to use these tools are barely able to move about in society without experiencing them.

But it wasn't always this way. In fact, the scene I've just described is not taken from the log of a modern astronaut but from one of the early scenes in the classic 1968 science-fiction film *2001: A Space Odyssey*.[1] The film, directed by Stanley Kubrick and based on a story by novelist Arthur C. Clarke, is a dazzling vision of the then-future. That scene is the work of moviemakers; it's a visual effect, and audiences who saw the film knew it. They knew that the idea of a man who could merely punch a few buttons, see his daughter on another planet, and speak to her in perfect real-time was just make-believe, as was the artificial intelligence HAL 9000 who plays the movie's most important role. In 1968, these were merely futuristic dreams on the silver screen.

Today we put those dreams in cheap cases and keep them in our pocket. Today those futuristic visions get plugged in to charge by our bedside every night. Today nearly everything from our work to our school, our hobbies, and even our church depends on what was once movie magic. We don't only take such things for granted; we get frustrated when they don't work as quickly, as clearly, or as efficiently as we think they should. They're such a part of our day that we get neck- and backaches from looking at them. We even develop psychological tics that

---

1 *2001: A Space Odyssey*, directed by Stanley Kubrick (Los Angeles: Metro-Goldwyn-Mayer Studios, 1968).

make us think these futuristic machines are talking to us when they're really not.[2]

It's an astonishing thought that a piece of movie magic from sixty years ago would have already become so routine. Our technological world has changed in ways and at a speed that no other era of human civilization could comprehend. And the vast majority of us cannot even fully describe our own world. Most of us are like the comedian who joked that if he were transported back to the Middle Ages, he would announce to the people that smartphone and internet technology were possible, and when they asked how such tools worked, he would say, "I have no idea." It's funny because it's true. We really don't comprehend our own world. We are much like the fish in David Foster Wallace's fable who don't know what "water" is. We've swum in its depths our whole lives and have no category for anything else.

Our inability to really comprehend the technological revolution that has permanently altered nearly all of our lives is a profound spiritual, emotional, and cultural dilemma. Digital technology merely from the last thirty years has transformed Western society thoroughly and quickly, but our fundamental response has been mostly to just go with it. We buy the latest version, sign up for the freshest platform, stream the newest stuff. All the while many of us sense that our communities, our friends, and even we ourselves are somehow different because of all these screens and pixels. Our eye-strain headaches tell us something is different. Our lethargic desire to binge-watch tells us something is different. Our sense of anxiety and loneliness and isolation after a marathon of giving and receiving "Likes" tells us something is different. But we just don't

2   Elise Hu, "Phantom Phone Vibrations: So Common They've Changed Our Brain?," NPR, September 27, 2013, https://www.npr.org/.

have the ability to name it. We feel we understand our world less and less even as we have more and more access to it.

One reason why *2001: A Space Odyssey* is a powerful film is that its technological Eden eventually falls. The HAL 9000 computer that operates with godlike power over the astronauts' space mission turns against its human masters. In the end, Kubrick and Clarke imagine a world where humanity's inventions become inhumane. The world of *2001* is a divided world where technological sophistication has tried to conceal a lack of something the Bible tells us is far more important, something that really can help us live fully and humanely in this wondrous, often terrifying world—

Wisdom.

What Is Wisdom?

What is wisdom? Culturally speaking, we often identify wisdom as the ability to make correct decisions. Many times, wisdom and "getting the right answer" are treated as synonymous; thus, we get the notion of the "wisdom of the crowd," which refers to the increased likelihood of arriving at the right answer if you poll enough people. We also conflate wisdom with experience, speaking of people who have seen or done a lot as "wise" and admonishing the youthful to "wise up," i.e., to stop being naive or aimless. In any case, the idea of wisdom is frequently a relative concept. It measures someone's aptitude in navigating a particular task or particular problem.

When the Bible speaks of wisdom, it speaks a bit differently. Christian wisdom is holistic. It does not reduce to book or street smarts, nor is it merely the sum total of our lessons learned. Instead, Christian wisdom is about living a life that responds correctly to reality. In his helpful book *The Fear of the Lord Is Wisdom*, theologian Tremper Longman III describes biblical wisdom as containing three essential levels: the skill of living (practical), becoming a good person (ethical), and fearing God (theological).[3] All three ways of living are wise not only because they are commanded by an authoritative Creator; they are wise because they are responsive to objective realities in the world.

Practical wisdom is the art of being able to discern what's really going on in a relational, vocational, personal context. Particularly in the book of Proverbs (which, along with Job and Ecclesiastes, makes up a part of Christian Scripture known as "wisdom literature"), a truly wise person is someone who can discern the right course of action in a puzzling or tense situation. Longman describes this wisdom as "similar to what today we often call emotional intelligence. . . . Emotionally intelligent people, like the wise in the book of Proverbs, know how to say the right thing at the right time. They do the right thing at the right time."[4] In other words, while others misinterpret reality and do or say something unfit for the moment, the wise person can "read the room," looking past surface appearance and seeing people and problems for what they really are.

This wisdom requires more than memorized idioms and platitudes. It requires a living knowledge of what people and the world are really like. Someone armed with only aphoristic knowledge of human nature will offer advice to a friend that backfires spectacularly, because that advice is not actually rooted in awareness of objective reality. People who are enslaved to their impulses will make decisions that get them in deep trouble because their emotions make them indifferent to the facts of the situation. To be wise is to live daily life in light of reality.

---

3 Tremper Longman III, *The Fear of the Lord Is Wisdom: A Theological Introduction to Wisdom in Israel* (Grand Rapids, MI: Baker, 2017), 6–25.

4 Longman, *Fear of the Lord*, 7.

This kind of wisdom doesn't stop at emotional intelligence, however. To live in light of reality also has a moral dimension, what Longman calls the "ethical level" of wisdom. If there really is such a thing as right and wrong, if objective moral standards are real in our universe, then a wise person must live in light of that truth as well. A desire to succeed at life is not enough. We have to be shaped in light of the reality of virtue.[5]

It was not that long ago that many in Western society believed that any talk of "objective morality" was misguided at best, despotic at worst. The philosophy of postmodernism was supposed to annihilate any appeal to universal ethical standards. "What's true for you is true for you, and what's true for me is true for me." But moral relativism has fallen on hard times, even—perhaps especially—among those who reject Christianity. Even the most committed relativists now will quickly agree that racial injustice is always wrong, or that violence and prejudice against women or LGBTQ+ people must not be tolerated in a just society. The contemporary West has rediscovered what the Bible never forgot: objective standards of right and wrong are woven into the very fabric of our existence. We cannot be fully human without them.

The third level of biblical wisdom according to Longman is theological. We will say much more about this particular level in a moment. For now, we can summarize the theological level of wisdom precisely the way the book of Proverbs summarizes it: "The fear of the LORD is the beginning of knowledge; fools despise wisdom and instruction" (Prov. 1:7). Even after we try to discern

---

5   Longman, *Fear of the Lord*, 11. Longman cites biblical scholar S. M. Lyu's work *Righteousness in the Book of Proverbs*, where Lyu writes, "Proverbs instructs that the reader should learn and become wise and righteous. To reach that goal, the learner is expected to go through the reshaping of his inner person. His desires, hopes, and disposition must be reconditioned to reflect the ideal."

the objectively true path forward in everyday life and the virtuous standard to which we need to conform, there remains the most fundamental aspect of wisdom. Wisdom fears the Lord. Holistic wisdom looks at reality and sees its author, majestic and sovereign and worthy of loyalty. As Longman writes, "the 'fear' of the 'fear of the Lord' is the sense of standing before the God who created everything, including humans whose every continued existence depends on him. The emotion is appropriate for wisdom because it demonstrates acknowledgment that God is so much greater than we are."[6] In this sense, the baseline of true wisdom is the ability to see God for who he is and, so seeing, to respond in the only reasonable way. God is not an idea. He is not a philosophical thesis to be contemplated in a merely theoretical way. God is everywhere. He is omnipresent, omniscient, and omnipotent. He is the only Creator and the only sustainer of that creation. He is the supreme sovereign over absolutely everything in our universe and any other. As the title of a famous book elegantly puts it, *He Is There and He Is Not Silent.*[7]

The essence of true wisdom, therefore, is to live fully aligned with ultimate reality: practical, ethical, and theological. To the extent that anyone is wise, he sees himself, the world around him, and God for what they truly are. As I remember one preacher putting it, a wise life is lived with, not against, the grain of reality that God has created.

"Sounds great," you may be thinking. "What does this have to do with digital technology?"

The answer to this question is the point of this book. If we want to live wisely according to Scripture, then we have to live in

---

6 Longman, *Fear of the Lord*, 12.
7 Francis A. Schaeffer, *He Is There and He Is Not Silent* (Carol Stream, IL: Tyndale, 1972).

alignment with reality. Yet throughout Scripture and throughout human history, fallen, sinful people have used technology to try to invent an alternative reality for themselves, a reality meant to "liberate" them from the fear of the Lord and conformity to his revealed character.

From the Tower of Babel to the golden calf, from the slave ships in the Atlantic to the crematoriums of the Third Reich, humans have tried from time immemorial to utilize their ingenuity to manufacture a different world with a different story than the one the Creator made. As we will see later, it is not just that we take neutral tools and use them in sinful ways. It's that the tools themselves can bend our vision of reality. In fact, to the degree that our "tools" not only alter how we experience God's world but begin to *distort* it, they become something other than tools. They become idols.

It is important to say at this point that this is not an antitechnology book. That we can craft and use tools that help us distort God and his reality is ultimately attributable to sin, not the material in the physical world that gave us the technology. The Bible is clear that God is completely sovereign over absolutely every molecule in the universe and that the material qualities of straw, wood, iron, gold, and silicon are what they are because God created them, and their very nature glorifies him.[8] Yet it is simultaneously true that because human beings are divine image bearers with a cosmic mandate to subdue the earth and represent God's rule on it (Gen. 1:27–28), our technology is massively theologically significant. We not only shape technology; technology shapes us. And certain *kinds* of technologies shape us in certain profound ways.

---

8   See Tony Reinke, *God, Technology, and the Christian Life* (Wheaton, IL: Crossway, 2022).

To live wisely is to live "with the grain" of the truth that a real God has revealed to us, but our computer-generated experience of life affects how well we can see and perceive (and thus, how well we can live according to) that truth. Stories have intrinsic power to change our lives. From the narratives of Scripture, to the ancient bards spinning mythical legends, to the great literature and drama and cinema of the modern world, stories captivate us at a level deeper than intellectual argument. As human culture transforms, so too do the stories we tell ourselves. And as we will see a little later, it is not simply the content of the stories that can captivate and change us but the form of these stories. *How* we hear can be just as powerful as *what* we hear.

In the online age, our default is to lose touch with reality. Left to ourselves and our machines, we find that wisdom often looks foolish, virtue often looks evil, and God often feels invisible. Every person living in a modern, digitally connected culture is constantly inhabiting a moral and intellectual habitat that distorts the biblical story of reality.

Perhaps this feels like overstatement. Sure, we all have the vague sense that we're too distracted by our phones or our apps. We wish we could read more and scroll less. But perhaps this is just a problem of time management. If we were just more disciplined or more productive, perhaps our digital immersion would be to our benefit rather than detriment. Maybe what we need are simply better corporations that will produce better and safer content for us to consume. Maybe the answer is that there is no answer, and it's time to stop worrying so much about it.

But the problem goes deeper than this. It's not just that our hyperconnected world consumes too much of our time and we need better techniques to rein it in. It's that many of these technologies fundamentally alter our perception of reality. As we'll see later, the kind of digital technologies that we carry around in our pocket and look at aimlessly throughout the day are shaping all of us into particular kinds of thinkers, whose thoughts are formed in the pattern of those technologies. In other words, we are learning to look at reality and see something different from what is actually there.

If the essence of wisdom is living in light of reality, our digital habitats can undermine wisdom by cutting us off (in small but real ways) from that reality. To see this, though, we cannot start by looking at the technologies themselves. The only way to know for sure if a poorly tinted window has been obscuring our vision of the yard is to know what the yard actually looks like. We have to see what's on the other side of the glass clearly. Only then will the flaws in the glass itself become apparent for what they are.

Before we interrogate the digital technologies that shape us, we need to know what kind of shape we are supposed to have as humans. The Reformer John Calvin began his *Institutes of the Christian Religion* by observing, "Our wisdom, insofar as it ought to be deemed true and solid wisdom, consists almost entirely of two parts: the knowledge of God and of ourselves."[9] To be wise, we need to see ourselves for what we really are, and we can do this in light of God's word.

A Theology of Embodiment

When we look to Scripture to discover what we human beings truly are like, one of the first, most foundational things we discover is that *we are embodied creatures made in the image of God.* Every part of that description is important. Humans are made in the image of

---

9 John Calvin, *Institutes of the Christian Religion*, trans. Henry Beveridge (Peabody, MA: Hendrickson, 2008), 1.1.1.

God, reflecting his nature, representing him, and reigning on his behalf over the earth and animal kingdom. We are also creatures. We are objects of God's creative work, and as such, we exist in a permanent state of dependence on and submission to him. God is Creator, we are creatures, and this order will never be reversed. Our status as creatures does two things. It limits our power and authority as we realize that we creatures need God and he does not need us. Second, it bestows astonishing dignity and honor on us because we are neither accidents nor mistakes that happened in nature.[10]

Many evangelical Christians could probably explain in some capacity why it matters that humans are creatures made in the image of God. What is harder for many of us is explaining why it matters that we are *embodied*. Of course, no one disagrees *that* we are embodied (at least not yet). But the fact of our having bodies does not seem to carry a lot of significance for many Western people today. In fact, it's easy to get the impression of the opposite, that many of us see our embodiment as an obstacle to be overcome, a limitation to be transcended, or even a necessary evil to be suppressed.

As theologian John Kleinig has observed, "society as a whole does not know what to make of the body."[11] Kleinig points out that many modern people express confusion about the body through one of two ways. First, they become "obsessed" with achieving a body they desire, so they go to great lengths to get slimmer, fitter, stronger, or prettier. Kleinig sums up the situation: "My ideal self, the person I would like to be, must match that ideal body. Yet that ideal is never fixed. It changes as fashions change."[12] The result

---

10 For an excellent introduction to this idea, see Anthony Hoekema, *Created in God's Image* (Grand Rapids, MI: Eerdmans, 1994).

11 John Kleinig, *Wonderfully Made: A Protestant Theology of the Body* (Bellingham, WA: Lexham Press, 2021), 5.

12 Kleinig, *Wonderfully Made*, 6.

for many people, however, is a profound and often debilitating shame over the way their body fails to look like the ideal body. This shame is expressed through an increasing alienation from our bodies, as we despair of having the image we desire and try harder and harder to separate our "inner self" from our disappointing physical self.

This dynamic that most of us experience—this connection we feel between our bodies and an ambient sense of shame or disappointment—is very near the center of the biblical story of the fall. After Adam and Eve sinned against God, their eyes were opened to the knowledge of good and evil. What did they see? They saw their naked bodies (Gen. 3:7). Their sin did not disrobe them; it did not free up their true selves, suppressed by fellowship with God. Instead, sin turned them *against* their true selves. The first experience of shame in the history of the world was between Adam and Eve and their own bodies.

Sin's power is visible not just in its capacity to alienate us from our bodies but to make this alienation the fundamental thing we are aware of when it comes to them. Because of this, we miss the good givenness of our bodies. By "good givenness" I mean the sheer reality that we exist in an embodied state and cannot do otherwise. Our bodies are given to us in our mother's womb. We are passive recipients of God's creative work. Even thousands of years before ultrasound technology, King David of Israel knew that the Lord had knit him together in his mother's womb and that the result was a body "fearfully and wonderfully made" (Ps. 139:14). What did David do to possess such a wonderfully made body? Absolutely nothing. His body was made for him without his input, without his effort, and without his agency, yet it is inarguably real and essential. The body has *givenness*.

Why does this matter? How does acknowledging the good given-ness of the body do anything for us in a digital age? The answer is found in the discussion of wisdom above. We've seen now that the wise life is the life lived in light of true reality. The material world in general and our bodies in particular are part of that reality. Our bodies, in their good givenness, are a fundamental aspect of who we are as people made in God's image. Therefore, true wisdom requires us to live within and accept our physical embodiment. Our creaturely design is divinely ordered, something to inspire worship, gratitude, and joy. Biblically speaking, it's when we attempt to get around or beyond our identity as embodied creatures that we plunge headlong into despair and folly.

Perhaps somewhat paradoxically, our cultural moment in the modern West is profoundly hostile to the body. The internet, which dominates our lives as the primary medium through which we encounter most of the world, is an entirely disembodied habitat. Consequently, the internet trains our consciences to think of ourselves and the world in disembodied ways. We do not exist bodily online but through photos and videos that we carefully manipulate to construct a preferred identity. On social media, our "community" is not a room full of people physically present, whom we can reach out and touch, but a collection of usernames and avatars and timelines. This habitat itself tells us a story—a story that humans are not essentially people with flesh and blood, voices, and facial expression, but "users" whom we can sufficiently know from their words, profile pictures, and shares.

This is not just a minor tweak in how we think of what it means to be a human person. It is an intellectual and spiritual revolution. And there is much reason to think that a worldview of disembodiment has currently seized the reins of cultural power.

In 2022 Lia Thomas, who was born William Thomas, became the first openly transgendered "woman"[13] to win an NCAA Division-1 swimming championship.[14] The story became a hotbed of national controversy throughout the US, with progressive transgender activists celebrating Thomas's victory and other observers questioning how allowing a biological male to compete against females made any competitive or rational sense. Indeed, Thomas is merely one example, a symbol of a much larger transformation in Western society with regard to the relationship between biological sex and gender. In the span of a few years, transgenderism has gone from the very fringes of cultural consciousness to the mainstream, an astonishing revolution with radical implications in our politics, medicine, education, and parenting.[15]

How has the idea of a person being stuck in the "wrong body" become not just respected but orthodox in many circles? There are many legitimate answers, but this book offers an overlooked one: digital technology has recalibrated our worldviews and reshaped our consciences not to see the good givenness of our bodies. This isn't merely a problem of content; it's a problem of *form*. In other words, it's not simply that on social media and the web we read sentences that devalue the physical. Rather, the *nature* of online

---

13 Some Christians feel that putting transgendered people's gender identity in quotes or referring to them with their birth pronouns instead of their preferred pronouns is unnecessarily
hostile and offensive and that it is best to advocate for gospel truth as much as possible
without putting barriers between us and unbelievers. While I respect this perspective, I believe Christians have a responsibility to tell the truth about human identity and that this
responsibility requires us to insist on a biblical and natural definition of gender.

14 Carson Field, "Out of Left Field: Thoughts on Swimmer Lia Thomas and the State of
Women's Sports," *Abilene Reporter News*, March 21, 2022, https://www.reporternews.com/.

15 For more on how this happened, see Carl R. Trueman, *Strange New World: How Thinkers
and Activists Redefined Identity and Sparked the Sexual Revolution* (Wheaton, IL: Crossway,
2022).

presence itself powerfully reinforces the sense that we are not our bodies, that we have total control over our identity and our story, and that any threat to this feeling can and ought to be "deleted" so that we don't have to put up with it.

According to a vast amount of research, teens and young adults in contemporary American society feel significantly lonelier and more isolated than generations prior.[16] For many, friendship is an elusive art that seems to be slipping further and further away with each successive generation. Even worse, the emerging generation of adults in many economically developed parts of the world are failing to marry and start families, sometimes well into adulthood and sometimes completely.

Meanwhile, technologically speaking, it has never been easier in human history to "connect" with another person: to meet, get to know, and develop a relationship with someone even over vast distances. The trends of loneliness and unwanted solitude have not only resisted technological connectivity; they seem to have worsened alongside digital connectivity's ascent.[17]

The major argument of this book is that Christians can only understand and respond to these and other cultural shifts correctly if we understand them in the context of digital technology's undermining of biblical wisdom. Because wisdom is a submission to God's good and given reality, our immersion in computer and internet existence is a crisis of spiritual formation. Our digital

---

16 Vivian Manning-Schaffel, "Americans Are Lonelier Than Ever—but 'Gen Z' May Be the Loneliest," NBC News, May 14, 2018, https://www.nbcnews.com/. See also Sherry Turkle, *Alone Together: Why We Expect More from Technology and Less from Each Other* (New York: Basic, 2012).

17 See Jean Twenge, *iGen: Why Today's Super-Connected Kids Are Growing Up Less Rebellious, More Tolerant, Less Happy—and Completely Unprepared for Adulthood* (New York: Atria, 2017); and Turkle, *Alone Together*.

environments *dislocate* us, training us to believe and feel and communicate in certain ways that our given, embodied, physical environments do not. The more immersive and ambient the technology, the more extreme this effect.

But can technology really do this? Isn't it simply a neutral tool that can be used for good or bad?

The answer is complicated.

2

How Technology Shapes Us

CHRISTOPHER NOLAN'S 2010 film *Inception* tells a fictional story about a technology called "dream-sharing," invented at some indeterminate point in the future, that allows participants to enter into one another's dreams via their subconscious.[1] The main character, Cobb (played by Leonardo DiCaprio), is a professional "dream hacker" who is skilled at entering into people's dreams and navigating their subconscious to find valuable information. At the behest of a billionaire CEO, Cobb assembles an expert team of hackers to invade the mind of a rival business tycoon and plant in his mind the desire to break up his company.

The movie is a dazzling thriller, filled with spectacular action sequences and mind-bending visual effects. But it's also a subtly profound parable. Perhaps more so than any other major Hollywood movie before it, *Inception* is a genuinely insightful and disturbing meditation on the relationship between mankind and its technologies. As the film progresses and its main characters

---

1 *Inception*, directed by Christopher Nolan (Los Angeles: Warner Brothers, 2010).

develop, the dream-sharing device turns out to be a terrifyingly apt metaphor.

In the world of *Inception*, dream-sharing is not just a tool to invade someone else's mind; it's a way to construct one's own subconscious reality. With training, sleepers can learn how to change the content of their dreams at will. However, this intoxicating ability erodes the sleeper's sense of what's real and what is a dream. As the dreamers port more and more of their desires and memories into the dream environment, they become increasingly immersed in the world of the dream. Not only does this immersion confuse their sense of reality (with tragic consequences in the case of one character); it recalibrates their desires entirely.

In one of the movie's best scenes, the team visits a chemist who can make especially potent sedatives to allow for vivid and prolonged dream-sharing. The chemist takes the team downstairs, where they're led to a dimly lit room where dozens of people are sleeping, connected to dream-sharing devices. The chemist explains that these people come to his shop to take the sedative and spend hours every day dreaming together, as their subconscious selves construct an alternative life in their dreams. Stunned, the team asks, "They come here to fall asleep?" "No," comes the reply. "They come here to wake up. The dream has become their reality. Who are you to say otherwise?"

Inception works as an excellent science-fiction film, but even more importantly, it understands something fundamental about our technological society. Dream-sharing is fiction, but the near limitless ability to construct our own version of reality lies in our pockets or on our desks nearly every day. Much like the pitiable patients in the film, our relationship with these technologies has a way of causing us to desire digital sleep. As much as we might tell ourselves that we go to the internet and social media to be plugged into what's going on in the world, many times we're logging on to escape it.

The power of technology to shape us is something that many evangelical Christians have not considered nearly enough. Particularly in the digital age, evangelicals have often focused exclusively on the *content* that our TVs, computers, and smartphones deliver to us rather than the *form* by which that content is delivered. If we were to borrow computing language to make this distinction, we might say that American evangelicals have had a lot to say about cultural software but very little about cultural hardware. When it comes to discernment about what to watch or read or listen to, there's much theological thinking that can assist. But what if the way we watch or read or listen—the medium, not just the message—also requires discernment?

The Medium Is the Message

The cultural critic Marshall McLuhan famously declared that "the medium is the message."[2] McLuhan was referring to the epistemological and moral power of technology as not simply a tool to deliver some desired good but a means of reshaping society. In his book *Understanding Media: The Extensions of Man*, McLuhan illustrates the transformative power of technology by observing how the railway and the airplane both created different kinds of environments to support it:

> What we are considering here, however, are the psychic and social consequences of the designs or patterns as they amplify or

2 Marshall McLuhan, *Understanding Media: The Extensions of Man* (Berkeley, CA: Gingko Press, 2013), 29.

accelerate existing processes. For the "message" of any medium or technology is the change of scale or pace or pattern that it introduces into human affairs. The railway did not introduce movement or transportation or wheel or road into human society, but it accelerated and enlarged the scale of previous human functions, creating totally new kinds of cities and new kinds of work and leisure. This happened whether the railway functioned in a tropical or a northern environment, and is quite independent of the freight or content of the railway medium. The airplane, on the other hand, by accelerating the rate of transportation, tends to dissolve the railway form of city, politics, and association, quite independently of what the airplane is used for.[3]

The railway, according to McLuhan, transformed civilization by creating railway-shaped cities, railway-shaped work, and railway-shaped leisure. Once geographical distance was no longer an immutable, given part of people's lives and experiences, the way people thought about things like work, home, and even time itself was permanently changed. On a much more intense level, commercial flights have likewise "shrunk" our conception of the world. It's not simply that jet airliners travel thousands of miles because that's what we want them to do. Rather, the fact that jet airliners can travel thousands of miles is itself a transformational physical fact that has consequences for how we think about ourselves and the world.

Consider the clock. In his delightful book *About Time: A History of Civilization in Twelve Clocks*, David Rooney documents how timekeeping technology has consistently transformed society. Some ancient Romans ardently resisted the novelty of the sundial,

3   McLuhan, *Understanding Media*, 31–32.

cursing "that man who first discovered the hours."[4] As Rooney shows, timekeeping technology has always served philosophical and political purposes, imposing a certain kind of structure and worldview on its beholders. Whether this is a spiritual structure of piety expressed in chiming bells that call for hourly worship or an imperialistic reminder of one nation's dominance over another, expressed through imposition of time, the fact remains: "technology is never neutral, because objects are made by people with an agenda of some sort."[5]

Central heating is another example. Before furnaces pumped heat into every part of a house, most homes were dependent on fireplaces to keep warm during winter. If you were not wealthy, the odds were good that there was only one fireplace in your house, which meant that there was one location in your home that supplied heat, which consequently meant that all the members of the household tended to gather at the same spot to share warmth. The necessity of sharing space created the sharing of time together. By contrast, central heating and cooling enabled comfort throughout a house. Technology literally decentralized homelife, laying the technical foundation for the everyone-has-their-own-bedroom layout of a home that we assume today. This architectural transformation has brought with it a philosophical transformation: an emphasis, for example, on granting children "privacy" and "respecting their space" that has had significant implications for parenting and the governance of the home.

What about the automobile? Henry Ford's assembly line gave the world not just a far more efficient way of traveling; it gave the

---

4 David Rooney, *About Time: A History of Civilization in Twelve Clocks* (New York: Norton, 2021), 11.
5 Rooney, *About Time*, 223.

world a new way of imagining itself. As one author explains, most of the twentieth century was defined by "the expectation that people would get from one place to another only by driving an automobile."[6] The speed and convenience of the automobile gave birth to a different way of thinking about our relationship to work, to home, and to each other. For most people before the nineteenth century, the concept of "place" carried a thick givenness: the place you were born was very likely the place you would live. Home was an inheritance, and vocation was downstream from place. The Industrial Revolution in transportation redefined the concept of space, and in so doing redefined the concept of home. Thanks to technology, the remote was now accessible, which meant you were free to structure your life around pursuing the best-paying job, the most prestigious education, the most exciting new town—or simply to just get away.

I should be quick to point out that these are not necessarily moral criticisms of the technologies. Hardly anyone who studies the history of clocks, air-conditioners, or automobiles desires to return to a world without them. Indeed, biblically speaking, pining for such a return is not an example of wisdom but of futility (Eccl. 7:10). The idea that technology changes the kind of people we are is not itself an argument against them; it's simply a true observation of the world we live in.

Further, evaluating these effects is enormously complicated, not least because the effects are subtle and sometimes almost impossible to notice. The medical doctor and philosopher Stanley Joel Reiser, for example, has made a provocative case that the stethoscope, along with other medical technology, made physicians less dependent

---

6   Eric Jacobsen, *Three Pieces of Glass: Why We Feel Lonely in a World Mediated by Screens* (Grand Rapids, MI: Brazos Press, 2020), 141.

on (and ultimately less interested in) the subjective experiences of patients. "As the physician makes greater use of the technology of diagnosis," he writes, "he perceives his patient more and more indirectly through a screen of machines and specialists. . . . These circumstances tend to estrange him from his patient and from his own judgment."[7] This isn't as simple as deciding whether a stethoscope or EKG machine is good or bad. Rather, the point is that technologies, simply by virtue of what they do, communicate something. They communicate a vision of what life *should* be like, what human beings and the natural world *should* be capable of.

Evangelical Christians in the West today sense that the ambient culture has changed dramatically over the past few decades. The moral language that was commonplace in schools, workplaces, and town halls just fifty years ago is not only absent but considered hateful, even treasonous. We know this, and our preaching, teaching, writing, and evangelism often reflect a sober awareness of our post-Christian situation. At the same time, however, many evangelicals struggle to understand how the situation has been transformed so quickly. Ideas about gender identity that were strictly the domain of far-left bastions in higher education just a decade ago are now topics of conversation among pastors and parents in middle America.

How in the world did we get here so soon? I believe an important answer is about technology. The epistemological and ethical effects of technology have gone underreported in evangelical spaces partially because *we don't know* how these material devices are shaping us, which in turn is due to a lack of a viable theology of spiritual formation. Just as timekeeping, heating, and automobile technologies created social and political revolutions because of what they

---

7   Stanley Joel Reiser, cited in Neil Postman, *Technopoly: The Surrender of Culture to Technology* (New York: Vintage, 1993), 101.

empowered people to be and do, so also has internet technology cultivated a spiritual revolution by its very form.

What Technology Is Saying

The idea of digital technology's sparking a spiritual revolution is not at all a novel or reactionary concept. In fact, there's good reason to believe such a holistically transformative effect was what the original visionaries behind personal computing always hoped. In his fascinating book *World Without Mind*, journalist Franklin Foer begins by narrating the history of personal computing, starting with the story of Stewart Brand. Brand, whom Foer refers to as a "crown prince of hippiedom," was a true child of the 1960s who rejected his parents' middle-class values and instead sought authenticity and higher truth through drugs, counterculture, and technology.[8]

Brand's New Age inclinations combined with his interest in digital technology to create a techno-utopianism. Brand believed that although "politics failed to transform, computers just might."[9] Brand favored life among the "free love" communes that had shown up in the latter half of the sixties, and he tried to imagine ways to use his interest in cutting-edge technology to help his friends become more self-actualized and liberated. The biggest result of this effort was *The Whole Earth Catalog*, published in 1968. "The catalog pointed readers toward calculators and jackets and geodesic domes, as well as books and magazines," Foer writes. "The goods themselves were less important than the catalog's theoretical arguments about them."[10]

---

8 Franklin Foer, *World Without Mind: The Existential Threat of Big Tech* (New York: Penguin, 2017), 12–13.
9 Foer, *World Without Mind*, 13.
10 Foer, *World Without Mind*, 18–19.

What were those arguments? A paragraph from the catalog summarizes its worldview thus:

We are as gods and might as well get good at it. So far, remotely done power and glory—as via government, big business, formal education, church—has succeeded to the point where gross defects obscure actual gains. In response to this dilemma and to these gains a realm of intimate, personal power is developing—power of the individual to conduct his own education, find his own inspiration, shape his own environment, and share his adventure with whoever is interested. Tools that aid this process are sought and promoted by the WHOLE EARTH CATALOG.[11]

In another world, *The Whole Earth Catalog* might have been just a piece of deep trivia from a colorful and chaotic chapter in American history. But it was much more than that. For one thing, the catalog was a massive success, selling millions of copies and winning prestigious literary awards. More importantly, the catalog expressed a philosophy of transhuman liberation through technology that shaped the foundation of the modern computing industry. "The Whole Earth Catalog is a foundational text of Silicon Valley," Foer writes. It "transposed the values of the counterculture into technology" and cast a vision for computers to be vehicles of "personal liberation and communal connection."[12]

The liberative vision of Brand and his catalog became influential not just with the general mass of tech-curious hippies on the West Coast, but also with some particular individuals who would go on to shape the digital world. One of the catalog's eager readers was a

---

11 *Whole Earth Catalog*, cited in Foer, *World Without Mind*, 19.
12 Foer, *World Without Mind*, 21.

young Steve Jobs. A computer engineer named Ray Kurzweil also caught the vision of technology-as-salvation and formulated the notion of the "Singularity," an eschatological belief that eventually human consciousness and technology will merge and form a new era in human existence.[13] Google cofounder Larry Page hired Kurzweil in 2012 as their "leading futurist."[14]

How influential is the idea that technology will "successfully" splice human beings from their bodily limitations and usher in a techno-paradise? Perhaps more than you think. *Transhumanism* refers to a broad set of beliefs and ideas about the future of human-machine singularity. Transhuman philosophy, far from being a foil in science fiction novels or a theoretical "slippery slope," is rather a live worldview among serious educators and inventors. In his helpful book *Transhumanism and the Image of God*, Jacob Shatzer describes the perspective of transhuman theorists: "By applying technology to ourselves, we can move beyond and become something that is posthuman."[15] The opening of the 1998 Transhumanist Declaration makes the connection between technology and the abolition of embodied limitation explicit: "Humanity stands to be profoundly affected by science and technology in the future. We envision the possibility of broadening human potential by overcoming aging, cognitive shortcomings, involuntary suffering, and our confinement to planet earth."[16]

A more detailed look at transhumanist philosophy is beyond the scope of this book. The point is that, historically speaking, our

13 Foer, *World Without Mind*, 47.
14 "Guess How Much Google Futurist Ray Kurzweil Spends on Food That Will Make Him Live Forever?!," *Business Insider*, April 13, 2015, https://www.businessinsider.com/.
15 Jacob Shatzer, *Transhumanism and the Image of God: Today's Technology and the Future of Christian Discipleship* (Downers Grove, IL: InterVarsity Press, 2019), 41.
16 "Transhumanist Declaration," cited in Shatzer, *Transhumanism and the Image of God*, 48.

computer and internet technologies express a worldview that was programmed into them at the outset. As Foer notes, this eschatological vision of technological transcendence permanently shaped the character of Silicon Valley's technology companies. It's evident not just in history but in the present.

Facebook cofounder Mark Zuckerberg believes the metaverse—an immersive virtual reality environment where digital renderings of people gather—is an essential step in the human journey toward total freedom to customize our bodies and our environment.[17] Elon Musk, as of this writing one of the wealthiest people in the world, has observed that as our personal computing tools become more important in our daily lives, the line between self and software is blurred. Musk welcomes an imminent chapter in human history where we will "see a closer merger of biological intelligence and digital intelligence."[18] Musk's point is that our existing relationship with digital technology makes such a transformation plausible. He's right. There's a vision of humanity, the good life, and our final destination as persons expressed not only by propositional language (i.e., statements that argue for these philosophies) but by these tools themselves. Once again, this doesn't mean that these technologies are inherently evil in themselves or that the right response would be to disavow permanently any use of computers or the web. Instead, what we must do if we want to live wisely in the world God has made is identify these ideas and worldviews for what they are, and understand how they can shape and move us even when we are not conscious of any mental battle going on.

---

17 Alex Heath and Nilay Patel, "Mark Zuckerberg Is Still All-In on Building the Metaverse," *The Verge*, October 11, 2022, https://www.theverge.com/.

18 "Elon Musk Says the Future of Humanity Depends on Us Merging with Machines," *Science Alert*, February 15, 2017, https://www.sciencealert.com/.

This glance at the intellectual heritage of much of our online and computer technology helps make sense of why these devices seem to powerfully separate us from the givenness of the world. In a very real sense, this is precisely what such technology was intended to do. Its function is downstream from a particular belief system, a story of humanity wherein salvation consists of overcoming givenness itself, curating a custom existence, and achieving freedom from boredom, limitation, ignorance, and even death.

Of course, simply because an invention's maker holds certain beliefs does not necessarily mean that the invention itself is synonymous with those beliefs. The doctrine of common grace prevents us from seeing human beings as simply the sum total of their worldview. Even parents who are evil can give good things to their children (Luke 11:13). The question is not whether a certain technology is tainted by an inventor's ideology; the question is whether we can see evidence of that ideology *in the way the invention works.* As we observed earlier, technologies, from the clock to the jet airplane, can create systemic changes in society so that people begin to think and feel and act in ways that are permanently shaped by those changes. Technology can recalibrate our vision of God's world. The question is not whether this happens; the question is which technologies do this, and how they do it.

If so, then when we look closely at the most important digital technologies of our time—especially the internet—we should expect to see traces of this posthuman vision. We should detect some kind of intrinsic tension between the given reality our bodies inhabit and the world that is rendered for us on the screen. We should expect to see that these "digital liturgies" don't just encourage us to try to escape from the givenness of God's world but that they actually obscure and resist that givenness in the very things they do.

And that's exactly what we find.

The Haze

Let me tell you about two friends of mine. I've known Dean and Erica for several years.[19] They don't know each other, and, in fact, I doubt they would have very much in common if they ever did meet, beyond the fact that they're both Christian, married, thirty-something parents of young children. Dean is a professional in online communications, specializing in helping people grow their digital platforms. Erica is a stay-at-home mother. Dean is fairly described as politically left of center. Erica is very conservative. Dean's kids attend public school, while Erica homeschools her children. In terms of ideological instincts, temperament, and where each is willing to err, Dean and Erica are two very different kinds of thinkers.

But over the last few years, I've noticed (and my wife has noticed) that something seems to have changed with both Dean and Erica. Although their social and political worldviews are far apart, both Dean and Erica seem to have changed in ways that are remarkably similar. For one thing, we've noticed that Dean and Erica seem to be very different kinds of people when we're talking to them in person and when we're reading their social media timelines.

In person, Dean is quite approachable and humble, easy to talk to, and seems open to considering viewpoints not his own. Online, however, Dean appears to be leaning much further into a theologically and politically progressive mindset, a mindset that seems to imply that people who don't agree with him are harmful and should be avoided. Dean is quite critical online toward certain doctrines or church practices that he was open to just a few years ago. What's more, Dean often "likes" or "shares"

19 These are pseudonyms.

content that he surely knows friends like me would find extremely controversial, perhaps even attacking. Yet this seemingly does not create awkwardness when we hang out. In fact, if all I knew from Dean was the way he talked outside social media, I would never have imagined him to feel this way at all. It's not his conversation but his posts that express skepticism toward evangelicals like me. When we talk about the gospel and our families over lunch, there's no eye-rolling, no snarky retorts, and certainly no heated arguments. We may not always agree, but the aggressive spirit that I pick up from him online is simply not there, and he doesn't seem to try to create it. In fact, it's almost like it's not the same person at all.

Something very similar has been going on with Erica. Erica is genuinely sweet and compassionate. In person, she still asks questions about how we're doing, checks on our kids, and keeps us up-to-date with everything going on in her family. She exudes friendliness and cheerfulness almost all the time. But online is a different story. Recently Erica has been far more strident and absolutist in her opinions about everything from vaccines to child safety. Even on issues that are not clearly addressed in Scripture, Erica has been projecting a kind of agitated confidence that is very surprising when compared to her offline persona. Interestingly, the opposite is true online: she has become less surprising. She has started to talk about certain issues in a very predictable way, often sounding exactly like certain opinion "influencers." It's not just that her opinions have become more plentiful online. They've become less thoughtful and more reactionary. Most distressingly of all, Erica seems less and less comfortable in offline conversations and visits. She'll come off as stressed and distracted, even meekly asking for prayer that the Lord would help her in a chaotic season of life. When we check her page, though, there's no sign of any stress or neediness. Her pictures show only smiling faces, happy times, and of course, correct opinions.

These changes in Erica and Dean might be easier to understand if they were more radical. People can certainly change. But what makes these transformations hard to comprehend is that they're really not radical. As far as I can tell, there's been no major change in their theology or worldview, there's been no significant life event that rattled their presuppositions, and (again, as far as I can tell) there's been no relational trauma or disillusionment that might have led to this palpable sense of conflict. What has happened instead is that Dean and Erica, while *what* they say is very different, are both thinking and speaking in a *new kind* of way. And that new kind of way feels distinctly like an internet-shaped way.

This might sound awfully self-righteous. But, truthfully, the real reason I've been concerned about Dean and Erica's recent transformation is that I've seen it in myself too. Everything I've just described about my friends is something I've picked up going on in my own mind and heart, and just like Dean and Erica, it's only gotten worse and more noticeable over the last few years. I think differently than I used to. I concentrate less and emote more. I value carefully reflecting on things, but what I end up doing a lot is simply seeing what people I dislike are saying and confidently taking the opposite position, whatever it is. Conversation is harder, reading is much more of a slog, and mental busyness is so alluring I almost feel restless when I'm *not* distracted. When I share these experiences with friends and family, almost everyone agrees that some version of this is happening to them. All of us seem to feel like we're in some kind of spiritual and intellectual haze.

47

What's happening? The answer, I believe, brings us back to that haunting scene in the film *Inception*. When people accept dreams as their reality, they feel like they have to go to sleep in order to wake up. In the movie, a dreamer's ability to construct his own reality is a two-way street: the dreams shape him into something different as well. That's true. What we choose to see as our reality changes us in that "reality's" image. The spiritual and intellectual haze we feel is the feeling of thinking, feeling, and believing more like our technologies. We are becoming what we worship.[20] And what we are worshiping has a mind of its own.

20 G. K. Beale, *We Become What We Worship: A Biblical Theology of Idolatry* (Downers Grove, IL: IVP Academic, 2008).

3

Drowning in the Shallows

AS SOON AS HE COULD swing a plastic bat, my son Charlie wanted to go outside and play baseball. In terms of a backyard, our small but comfortable condo in suburban Chicago had a plot of grass about the size of our hallway bathroom. But the confines were friendly. From the age of three, all Charlie wanted to do on a sunny spring day was stand on that plot of grass and swing as I pitched. All parents believe their children are especially talented at everything they try at that age, but I still have managed to convince myself that Charlie is a natural baseball player.

But one problem we ran into was that Charlie struggled with perseverance. If the swing wasn't connecting the first few times, he didn't want to keep practicing. In the first year or two of our backyard baseball games, Charlie would tolerate only a handful of pitches without a hit. My reminders that he had to practice in order to get better only made him more frustrated. Plenty of outdoor baseball adventures ended with no hits and many tears as he was unwilling to continue practicing what felt (to him) like a hopeless exercise.

You probably know where the story goes from there. Despite the tears, despite the frustration, Charlie slowly, incrementally, but meaningfully got better at hitting the ball. Every week of practice was a little better than the one before. And before he even knew what was happening, Charlie was making steady contact, consistently getting hits and fewer whiffs. Is there a more classically American tale of perseverance than a three-year-old with his baseball bat?

Repetition, as much as it exasperates, is important. It can make us better at something. It can make a person remember faster and recite better. But most amazingly of all, repetition can actually change the kind of people we are. It turns out that in God's providential design of our bodies, repetition has an astonishing power to reshape our minds, recalibrate our desires, and even redefine our beliefs. As we immerse ourselves in something time and time again, our thoughts, feelings, and intuitions begin to align with whatever that is.

Especially if that thing is the internet.

You Are What You Scroll

In August 2008, writer and researcher Nicholas Carr published an essay in *The Atlantic* entitled, "Is Google Making Us Stupid?" At the start of the essay, Carr offers a lament for his mind. It remains one of the most important paragraphs I've ever read:

> Over the past few years I've had an uncomfortable sense that someone, or something, has been tinkering with my brain, remapping the neural circuitry, reprogramming the memory. My mind isn't going—so far as I can tell—but it's changing. I'm not thinking the way I used to think. I can feel it most strongly when I'm reading. Immersing myself in a book or a lengthy article used to be easy. My mind would get caught up in the narrative or the

turns of the argument, and I'd spend hours strolling through long stretches of prose. That's rarely the case anymore. Now my concentration often starts to drift after two or three pages. I get fidgety, lose the thread, begin looking for something else to do. I feel as if I'm always dragging my wayward brain back to the text. The deep reading that used to come naturally has become a struggle.[1]

Carr's search to discover the cause for his mental distress led him to a revolutionary conclusion. The internet, which had become for Carr (like millions of others) the most normal, most immersive, most consuming medium of communication and learning, was changing his brain. Referring to the net as a "universal medium," Carr described it not simply as an extreme expansion of traditional written word tools but as something different entirely, something that, particularly through repeated immersion, shaped the human brain to be more net-like.

Two years after his essay appeared in *The Atlantic*, Carr expanded his argument into a book. *The Shallows: What the Internet Is Doing to Our Brains* makes a clear, persuasive, and important argument that the *form* of the web is a neurologically powerful tool for rewiring how human beings learn, feel, and process information. If Carr is correct, then it's not just the messages that we find on the web that influence us; it's the web itself, the process through which the web puts us as we engage its powers. As Marshall McLuhan put it, "The medium is the message."[2] And in the case of the web, it is one of the most powerful messages in the world.

1   Nicholas Carr, "Is Google Making Us Stupid?," *The Atlantic*, July/August 2008, https://www.theatlantic.com/.

2   Marshall McLuhan, *Understanding Media: The Extensions of Man* (Berkeley, CA: Gingko Press, 2013), 29.

Carr begins by unpacking cognitive research that demonstrates the human brain's "plasticity." This refers to the ability of our brain to make significant changes to itself: new neural patterns and different kinds of synapses that retrain our brain how to interpret input. "Every time we perform a task or experience a sensation, whether physical or mental," Carr writes, "a set of neurons in our brains is activated."

> If they're in proximity, these neurons join together. . . . As the same experience is repeated, the synaptic links between the neurons grow stronger and more plentiful through both physiological changes, such as the release of higher concentrations of neurotransmitters, and anatomical ones, such as the generation of new neurons or the growth of new synaptic terminals. . . . What we learn as we live is embedded in the ever-changing cellular connections inside our heads.[3]

That's an intimidating-sounding paragraph to most of us. But the point is simple enough: the human brain possesses within itself the capacity to change. The neural phenomena that are associated with one set of attitudes or behaviors can change into a different kind in response to repeated practices or consumption. In other words, our choices matter in shaping us into a certain kind of person. Carr concludes, "Our ways of thinking, perceiving, and acting, we now know, are not entirely determined by our genes. Nor are they entirely determined by our childhood experiences. *We change them through the way we live*—and . . . *through the tools we use.*"[4]

---

3 Nicholas Carr, *The Shallows: What the Internet Is Doing to Our Brains* (New York: Norton, 2010), 27.
4 Carr, *Shallows*, 31; emphasis added.

The plasticity of the brain helps to explain the phenomenon that we discussed in the previous chapter of how major technologies can create different kinds of societies that end up shaped around the technologies. Part of the reason this is true at a cultural level is that it is true at an individual level. New technologies do more than give us new ideas or methods; they can create new neural pathways in our brains that transform how we conceive and respond to reality. Carr cites political scientist Langdon Winner as saying, "If the experience of modern society shows us anything, it is that technologies are not merely aids to human activity, but also powerful forces acting to reshape that activity and its meaning."[5] In particular, Carr specifies that "intellectual technologies"—technologies that directly influence human language and thinking—communicate by their design and function certain ideas about "how the human mind works or should work."[6] In other words, our intellectual technologies are constantly preaching to us, and over time, their sermons transform how we think and act.

Carr's category of intellectual technologies is helpful for making distinctions between certain kinds of technology. A wheel, a rifle, and a jet airplane certainly reshape cultures through the possibilities they unlock and the vision of life we embrace as we use them. But this effect is significantly different from the effect that language-based tools have. Devices and practices that alter our habits of speaking and reading consequently alter our habits of learning and thinking. It is these technologies that tend to have the most power over us.

Talking about any technology this way may sound strange to you. Over the last few months, I've been asked many times what

5 Langdon Winner, cited in Carr, *Shallows*, 47.
6 Carr, *Shallows*, 45.

this book is about. When I tell someone that it's about the spiritually formative power of the web, I can almost always see a mixture of understanding and confusion in their faces. The confusion may owe to the fact that many evangelicals do not intuitively attribute spiritual significance to *things*. Objects, places, and other material realities don't seem morally or spiritually important. We tend to emphasize the limits of material things, what they are *not*. The church is *not* a building. God's word is *not* a leather-bound book (but the canonical words within that book). Our attention is fixed on the immaterial often to the exclusion of the material.

Yet a strict material/immaterial dualism is not what Christianity teaches. Neuroplasticity and the formative power of technology are profoundly theologically relevant because human beings, created in the image of God and belonging to God "body and soul,"[7] are irrevocably physical. While our bodies and souls are not equally central to our spiritual lives, our souls depend on our bodies,[8] which means that our spiritual lives—our pursuit of sanctification, of wisdom, and of virtue—are bodily lives too. What's more, habits and practices, while carried out externally by physical means, are spiritually significant because they shape us into particular kinds of people.

In Psalm 1, the blessed man is described as one who delights in the law of the Lord and meditates on it day and night (v. 2).

He is like a tree
 planted by streams of water
that yields its fruit in its season,

---

7 Heidelberg Catechism, Question 1 (1563), https://www.crcna.org/.
8 The human person cannot exist without a soul, but it can exist without a body. Nevertheless, humanity's destiny is embodiment.

and its leaf does not wither.
In all that he does, he prospers. (Ps. 1:3)

Here, spiritual blessedness is connected to the physical (neurological) practice of meditating on the law of the Lord with delight. To drive home the point, the psalmist compares the blessed, law-meditating man to a tree whose roots drink deeply of a rich stream. While the blessed man's relationship to God's word is certainly *more* than a physical matter of hearing and meditating on it, it is not *less*.

Carr's insights into the power of material things to change us resonate deeply with a Christian view of spirituality. In his book *You Are What You Love: The Spiritual Power of Habit*, James K. A. Smith makes the case that our conformity to the image of Christ is a process expressed through the formative effect of repeated actions and rituals:

> In our culture that prizes "authenticity" and places a premium on novelty and uniqueness, imitation has received a bad rap, as if being an imitator is synonymous with being a fake (think "imitation leather"). But the New Testament holds imitation in a very different light. Indeed, we are exhorted to be imitators. "Follow my example," Paul says, "as I follow the example of Christ" (1 Cor. 11:1). Similarly, Paul commends imitation to the Christians at Philippi: "join together in following my example, brothers and sisters, and just as you have us as a model, keep your eyes on those who live as we do" (Phil. 3:17). Like a young boy who learns to shave by mimicking what he sees his father doing, so we learn to "put on" the virtues by imitating those who model the Christlike life. This is part of the formative power of

our teachers who model the Christian life for us. It's also why the Christian tradition has held up as exemplars of Christlikeness the saints, whose images were often the stained glass "wallpaper" of Christian worship. . . . Such moral, kingdom-reflecting dispositions are inscribed in your character through rhythms and routines and rituals, enacted over and over again, that implant in you a disposition to an end (*telos*) that becomes a character trait—a sort of learned, second-nature default orientation that you trend toward "without thinking about it."[9]

In other words, becoming people more like Jesus involves far more than intellectual recall. We become more like Jesus as we give ourselves over to practices that push our hearts closer to him in love and trust. As we pursue these Christian habits of virtue in our lives, the Spirit uses them to bring about genuine change in our hearts. This is one of the major reasons that Christians throughout the years have held out the practices of Scripture reading, private prayer, and corporate worship as essential for spiritual growth. Intellectually speaking, many of these practices are highly repetitive. We read the same passages and pray the same kind of prayers and hear the same kind of sermons over and over again. If the essence of becoming more like Christ was attaining novel information, these repetitive practices would make little sense. But new information is not the point. It's not merely an issue of knowing the right things, but of having our hearts positioned in the direction of holiness.

But there's a dark side to this equation as well, and here's where we come back to Nicholas Carr and the formative power of the internet. Our habits drive certain values deep down in our hearts

---

9   James K. A. Smith, *You Are What You Love: The Spiritual Power of Habit* (Grand Rapids, MI: Baker, 2016), 18–19.

to change the kind of people we are. Physically, this change is very real because our brains are plastic and form new neural pathways in response to our behavior, and these pathways shape our desires and intuitions. The question then becomes, What happens to us if our habits are *not* positioning our hearts toward God's truth but toward something else? What if we are what we scroll?

The Internet as Epistemological Habitat

In *You Are What You Love*, Smith describes a place that actively trains our desires and beliefs in a certain direction: the shopping mall. Smith refers to the mall as a "temple," a secular sanctuary whose very nature preaches a gospel of consumerism. Every store in the mall, Smith observes, is offering a vision of the good life through its signs, models, appearance, and more. As we are inside, the power of this "gospel," expressed through the messages we read and physical designs we enter, becomes apparent. We find ourselves somehow agreeing with the mall that, yes, we would indeed be happier if we bought those shoes or that gadget. Yes, we have indeed been feeling ugly or lonely or bored lately, and these purchases would help us. Smith observes, "This is a gospel whose power is beauty, which speaks to our deepest desires. It compels us to come in, not through dire moralisms, but rather with a winsome invitation to share in this envisioned good life."[10]

The shopping mall's lights, music, models, and advertisements are designed to elicit a response inside us that the mere sight of the products themselves probably would not. In other words, the mall is an epistemological (and moral) habitat. It is an environment where buying more stuff becomes more plausible, where the

10 Smith, *You Are What You Love*, 43.

idea that happiness is a purchase away seems easy to believe and easy to act on.

Is the internet likewise an epistemological habitat? Carr argues that it is. "Because language is, for human beings, the primary vessel of conscious thought, particularly higher forms of thought," Carr writes, "the technologies that restructure language tend to exert the strongest influence over our intellectual lives."[11] The internet, Carr observes, is a medium unlike any other kind. It transforms the way words and ideas are expressed from one mind to another, and thus it transforms (to varying degrees) the meaning of language itself.

How does the internet transform language? Carr demonstrates that digital syntax is intrinsically different from the messages we take away from printed material. For one thing, the internet is "bidirectional," meaning that people can receive and send content through the same medium at the same time.[12] To read a book, newspaper, or personal letter is to encounter the meaning of words wholly as a recipient rather than a contributor. You can make notes in the margins or even throw the printed material in the garbage, but the words themselves are fixed in their medium, and it is impossible to "give back" to the medium in the same way.

The internet's inherent volatility as a medium is extremely important in shaping it as an epistemological habitat. Without physical material, we comprehend the meaning of language differently. In other words, the internet actually retrains us as readers. "When the Net absorbs a medium, it recreates that medium in its own image," writes Carr.[13] Practically speaking, this means that internet language comes to us already having been conditioned by the

11 Carr, *Shallows*, 50–51.
12 Carr, *Shallows*, 85.
13 Carr, *Shallows*, 90.

medium. One example is hyperlinks, which allow words on the internet to contain in themselves access to other words. If those other words also have hyperlinks, then they contain in themselves access to more words. This potentially endless rabbit-hole effect in digital language changes how we process information, evaluate claims, or reflect on ideas. "Links don't just point us to related or supplemental works; they propel us toward them. They encourage us to dip in and out of a series of texts rather than devote sustained attention to any one of them. Hyperlinks are designed to grab our attention. Their value as navigational tools is inextricable from the distraction they cause."[14]

To see just how significant this really is, a word picture might be helpful. Imagine that someone is reading an online article critiquing the pro-life worldview. The author argues that pro-life people are hypocritical, and writes this sentence: "For example, many pro-life people have no problem with brutal and cruel acts toward those who disagree with them." The reader notices that the phrase "brutal and cruel acts" is in blue font with underlining, meaning that these words contain a hyperlink to another page. She clicks the page and is promptly shipped off to a story on another website about a man who detonated a bomb in an abortion clinic. A very distressing story! About two paragraphs into the article, she sees a sentence, which is also clearly a hyperlink, about the perpetrator's connection to a church. She stops reading the article and clicks the new link. Off she's sent to *another* page, which is a homepage for the church. After clicking "About Us," she sees that the church is affiliated with a denomination, and she finds *another* hyperlink, which she clicks.

14 Carr, *Shallows*, 90.

Now imagine that this reader does not have any particularly strong views on abortion. Imagine further that this person has no journalistic training and is not used to interrogating articles for evidence of bias or fallacies. The reader will probably walk away from her hyperlink-jumping with an unclear idea of what pro-life people believe, who this bomber was, what kind of church that is, or what that denomination teaches. The reader will have a vague, hyperlink-shaped impression that associates the bomber with the pro-life movement, the church, and even the denomination. If she didn't finish the news story about the bombing before she clicked the hyperlink and was whisked away, she didn't see if there was a statement from the church condemning the violence and the bomber. Further, she might get the impression that the denomination has something to do with all this. Instead of reading, she has used hyperlinks to form a series of associations that feel like comprehension but are in fact just a type of distraction.

Hyperlinks are an example of how the web's form teaches us how to think (or how not to think). In the digital epistemological habitat, certain ideas and associations are plausible not because they make rational sense or are even accurately communicated, but because of how easily and seamlessly they are accessed.

Human attention is finite. There are limits to how well and accurately we can think when our attention is besieged with multiple stressors. This point is demonstrated compellingly by several studies cited by Carr that show an inverse correlation between the amount of multimedia in front of us and our ability to accurately remember and restate the information that multimedia was communicating. The problem, Carr observes, is not the presence of pictures or sound, both of which can be used to enhance comprehension and learning. The problem is rather the internet's unique, consciousness-bending format that trains our minds not to sit and reflect but to keep scrolling, keep skimming, and keep looking for a novel bit of information. Carr describes the internet as "an interruption system, a machine geared for dividing attention."[15]

The restlessness that many modern people feel when they are "unplugged" for a while is a restlessness that is built into many of our machines. As our brains become accustomed to nonstop input, surface-level engagement, and hurried scrolling from one bullet point to the next, the reality of neuroplasticity kicks in. The sensations of distraction and mental weightlessness become the new normal. What's more, the internet's most important and intrinsic features, such as search engines and algorithms, begin to think for us. As our attention span thins and our capacity for quality reflection diminishes, we begin to depend more and more on the web's tools of efficiency and attention-grabbing. We begin to think like the internet.

What Makes the Web Different

Before we move on, it might be a good time to answer a big question at the heart of this book, namely: How are the heart-shaping effects of the web meaningfully different from the heart-shaping effects of other things? For example, watching television likewise immerses us in stories, and most of the stories we encounter through TV are pressing us away from biblical wisdom instead of toward it. If what we need is to inhabit environments and practices that remind us of who God is and who we are as his embodied creatures, why not focus on the many other things that keep us from doing this? Why single out digital technology?

15 Carr, *Shallows*, 131.

The answer is closely connected to what Nicholas Carr uncovered about the web as a shaper of our minds. Ours is a thoroughly, relentlessly *digital* age. As mentioned earlier, the web has revolutionized nearly every aspect of our lives. How we learn, how we communicate, how we consume, and even how we worship as a society looks much different now than it did even forty years ago. Because of this, the web is quickly becoming more than just another epistemological or spiritual habitat that competes for our attention and presence. It is becoming the foundational medium, the superstructure of nearly every other experience.

We demand shorter and shorter books that will accommodate our diminished focus and present to us more like what we read online. We are becoming less tolerant of friends who voice opinions we dislike, so accustomed we are to being able to mute or delete that which discomforts us. We are becoming much more anxious, unable to accept stillness or silence that cuts against our daily intake of new noise. These real, offline effects emerge from our online habits because, in God's providential design, our minds are also brains—physical objects with pathways and neurons and adaptability.

The spiritually formative nature of the web is incredibly powerful precisely because it is so immersive and so assumed in our modern life, and we are becoming—physically and psychologically—different kinds of people because of it. And because Christian teaching will not let us divide what happens to our minds and affections from what happens to our spirits, the web's ability to reshape us as people becomes a spiritual ability. The values that the web imparts to us—the ones that we will see in the chapters ahead—color nearly every day of our lives, not to mention the social fabric of contemporary culture.

Very few people crave to be affected in these ways by their technologies. It's something that simply happens. Previously we observed that our technologies, especially internet technology, "speak" to us. How so? It communicates a vision of what we should be capable of, of what the good life really looks like. Just as the invention of a clock creates certain economic and social values (like punctuality), internet technology has a moral language that dictates certain other values. The moral language of our technologies is so easy to miss precisely because the technologies change the way we see them. We don't realize when we're being pushed toward rhythms, patterns, and attitudes that undermine Christian formation because we usually only look for that in explicit worldviews, not in our devices. But they are there.

The reality is that the default in much of Western culture is to rely on internet technology to fill the gaps in our minds and hearts. We don't know what we want to watch, so we click the "recommended" options. We don't know what we want to think about, so our social media filters deliver us the posts that are algorithmically the most likely to get us to respond. We don't know who our friends are, so we comb through the internet's "suggested follows," farming out our relationships to its technology. Our spiritual and intellectual menu is held by technologies that are designed not to help us savor what we find, but only to ensure that we binge, and then binge again.

Like the shopping mall, the internet is a heart habitat that makes its vision of the true, the good, and the beautiful more plausible to us. But what *is* that vision? The answer is nothing less than a set of digital liturgies.

PART 2

―――――――

ENGAGING THE
DIGITAL LITURGIES

THUS FAR, we've highlighted three important insights. First, part of faithfulness to God as embodied humans means living wisely, and this wisdom consists primarily of seeing the world the way God sees it and responding accordingly. We live wisely when we live along the grain of God's character, his law, and his creation. Consequently, anything that tilts us away from the givenness of reality—including but not limited to our physical existence as bodied creatures—undermines wisdom.

Second, part of what it means to be an embodied human is to be responsive in body and mind to the material world. We are shapable beings whose culture, habits, and worldviews form us into particular kinds of people. Internet technology communicates to us a vision of the good life, a narrative about who we are and what we should become. This narrative inclines our hearts toward a kind of disembodied utopianism, a latent belief (formed through habits) that through the right gadgets and techniques we can overcome our bodily limitations and even the constraints of being physical creatures. The more we are immersed in this technology, especially at an unconscious level, the more our desires, instincts, and ideas reflect this story.

Third, the internet is an especially powerful technology for creating these new patterns of belief and behavior in us. This is not merely an issue of the kinds of things we find online; it's an issue of the form of the internet itself. The web is an epistemological (knowledge-based) habitat that commends certain ways of thinking and not thinking. In particular, the web reteaches the human brain how to think, prioritizing shallow skimming and knee-jerk intuition over the slower discipline of contemplation. As the practices of online "learning" are repeated over and over again, our minds are quite literally transformed into internet-shaped minds. Because of this, certain values and ways of thinking become more plausible to us than they would be outside the epistemological habitat of the web. The web preaches to our brains and to our hearts.

So the question naturally becomes, *What* is the web preaching? That question is the theme of this next section of the book.

Like the church and the shopping mall, the web is a place of personal formation where certain behaviors and beliefs appear more desirable and plausible, and others appear less so. But unlike the church and the mall, the web—especially social media—has become a daily ritual for the vast majority of modern people. For many years, the internet was an "opt-in" medium, meaning that a normal person had to proactively seek out opportunity, sit in a particular room, and use a very specific set of skills to enjoy it.

Now, the internet has become "opt-out." Nearly by default, we are online. Our typical habits and rhythms are soaked with digital connectivity. To create a little bit of offline space, we have to pro-actively "opt-out" because the definition of normal has changed from offline to online.

If it's true that the web is an epistemological habitat that shapes us, then it is imperative that we are awake to this fact, because we will be within that habitat almost constantly. The question is not, Is this technology shaping me right now? The question is, *How* is this technology shaping me right now?

The second reason we need to know about the formative power of technology is that the *content* of media is always changing. We need something more than to be told that *X* website is wrong about *Y* issue, or that famous personality John Doe is not thinking biblically about this or that topic. Yet the tendency of evangelicals over the past few years has been to zero in on the content of digital media, to encourage one another to use discernment, filters, account-ability, and time limits. These things can be valuable, but a focus on content to the exclusion of form creates an illusion of purity.

You won't find many Christians on Facebook defending pornog-raphy, but how many times have you read a thread where believers were warring against each other, twisting words and angrily tearing their brothers and sisters down without even articulating the issues at hand? It would be absolutely shocking to see a pastor use obscene language to make a point in his sermon, but how shocking is it to log in to Twitter and see a pastor accusing someone he barely knows (or doesn't know at all!) of being a faithless heretic? When we see such contradictions, we might conclude that these Christians are phonies and that their online personas are "who they really are." But I'm convinced this would be mistaken. In many cases, it's not that such people are phonies but that they are deeply, fundamentally shaped by the values of the media they use.

When we look deeply into digital technology, we see habits, beliefs, and desires that are constantly forming us. These habits, beliefs, and desires constitute digital liturgies—ways of living that are centered on a vision of the good life. Now we are ready to see what those digital liturgies are and evaluate them in light of the life that our Creator has made for us.

4

"My Story, My Truth"

Digital Liturgy #1: Authenticity

JAMIE IS A COLLEGE STUDENT. His English literature class is currently studying the novel *The End of the Affair* by Graham Greene.[1] At one point in the discussion, the professor asks the class to consider Greene's point of view toward the adulterous relationship between Maurice and Sarah. This leads to a conversation about the merits of marital faithfulness and the perils of infidelity. Jamie doesn't have a strong opinion about the book. However, he does have a strong opinion about loveless marriages. His father and mother divorced when Jamie was twelve, and everyone in their family is (in Jamie's view) the better for it. Mom and Dad had fallen out of love, and their efforts to live together were just too stressful on the home. Life seems objectively happier for both Jamie's mother and father after the split. The idea that

---

1 Graham Greene, *The End of the Affair* (London: Heinemann, 1951).

Jamie's mom and dad—or any couple who've stopped loving each other—should have stayed together not only seems backward to Jamie but downright offensive.

Jamie raises his hand. He says that unlike many other people in the class, he has real experience in this area. Jamie says that he finds Greene's Roman Catholic views on marriage patriarchal and outdated, and that nobody could convince him as a child of divorce that staying in a hard marriage is better than having an affair or splitting up. Several students nod in agreement while a few others express some respectful pushback: Is divorce always the best option? Is breaking a marriage vow through adultery really the best way to help a family? One student mentions that she also is a child of divorce, and she wonders every day what life would have been like had her parents stayed together. Jamie has more he could say, but the professor, both for time and comfort's sake, moves the conversation onto less controversial ground.

To many observers, this exchange would probably have looked perfectly normal, an example of the kind of dialogue and debate that higher education is meant to cultivate. But inwardly Jamie is fuming as class is dismissed. He finds a table in the corner of the student cafe, gets his phone, and logs in to Twitter. In a tweet thread, Jamie tells his followers how a professor in his literature class allowed other students to trample all over him. He tried, he says, to tell his truth, but the professor was clearly sympathetic to religious zealotry and did not instruct the class to take Jamie's lived experiences seriously enough. Jamie ends his Twitter thread with a warning to others who might consider taking this professor or this class: prepare to have your story and your identity dismissed and ignored.

Just a couple minutes after publishing his tweets, Jamie's phone begins chirping. He's getting notifications, a lot of them, and they are all supportive. People are replying, "Ugh, I am so sorry this happened to you. Please know you are believed." Some are sharing Jamie's thread and adding, "Read this if you want to know what life is like for people like us at this school." Many are congratulating Jamie on telling his story despite the "obvious hostility" of the class. Dozens of notifications turn into hundreds, and soon Jamie has an online swarm of encouragement and support, mostly from people he doesn't know. A few students who've shared the thread begin asking how to register a formal complaint against the professor. After all, they reason, if he's willing to ignore Jamie's truth, won't he just ignore ours?

In one sense, the above story is fictional. The people, school, conversation, and tweets are not real (*The End of the Affair*, however, is real, and a novel you should read). But in another sense, this story is painfully genuine. It's a story that plays out on a regular basis on most American university campuses. Replace the name "Jamie" with a different name, replace Graham Greene's novel with a different book, and you could simply be retelling any number of news stories about colleges that have been rocked by student activism—activism that began, in many cases, with concern over someone's violation of "my truth."

In fact, these stories have become so common that there are now substantial books written about them. One of the best of these books is *The Coddling of the American Mind*, written by psychologist Jonathan Haidt and free-speech advocate Greg Lukianoff. Neither Haidt nor Lukianoff are Christians or conservatives. They don't advocate for biblical truth or traditional values. But Haidt and Lukianoff believe that contemporary university students are being weakened by ideologies that purport to protect individuals from ideas that may be uncomfortable to them. Teachers, counselors, and administrators, they argue, are undermining the intellectual fortitude and personal well-being of students by falsely assuming that (and then behaving as if) students are "fragile." "Even those who are not fragile themselves often believe that *others* are in danger and therefore need protection," Haidt and Lukianoff write. "There is no expectation that students will grow stronger from their encounters with speech or texts they label 'triggering.'"[2]

The authors offer a complex and nuanced explanation of why this culture of "fragility" came about. But the factor I want to reflect on most of all is the role that technology has played in shaping many people, especially millennials and younger, to be the kind of people who are likely to feel aggrieved or upset by disagreement. If we look hard at the epistemological habitat of the internet through the eyes of wisdom, we will see that the privileging of personal experience as ultimate truth is not just something we find online; it's the very logic of the social internet itself.

The Democratization of Everything

The internet, at least in one sense, is a radically egalitarian technology. As we considered earlier, the web empowers us to overcome the limits of our bodies and the natural world. Through the power of the web, we can charge right through the barriers of space (a videoconference with a coworker 5,000 miles away), time (instant written communication), and physical givenness (editing our online personas to be just right). Importantly, the web doesn't care whether a person is rich or poor, white or black, tall or short, male or female, famous or anonymous, incarcerated or free. The codes and algorithms that deliver the web to the world do not discrimi-

2   Jonathan Haidt and Greg Lukianoff, *The Coddling of the American Mind: How Good Intentions and Bad Ideas Are Setting Up a Generation for Failure* (New York: Penguin, 2018), 7.

nate. If you have the right technology, you can see, do, and become whatever you want.

Of all the web's achievements, one of its greatest is surely the sheer freedom of access to information it has given to billions of people around the world who would probably otherwise have never come near it. From my home office in south Louisville, Kentucky, I can gaze at ancient treasures of art and writing housed in the most elite museums around the world. In a matter of seconds, I can view a real-time street map of Paris, London, or Johannesburg, exploring side streets as I wander virtually. Research that until very recently was only possible for those with the time and resources to rifle through books and periodicals in physical libraries is now accessible to me almost as fast as I can think of it. How is it possible that a middle-class nobody like me could experience all of this? How can someone with (almost!) no money and no elite connections possess all this knowledge and resource? The answer, of course, is the web. The web has made world travelers, cultured observers, and knowledgeable artisans out of billions of us.

The word for this is *democratization*. Democratization is literally the *process of* democracy, or the process by which democracy emerges. When we say that the web has democratized information and experiences, we mean that it has made things that otherwise would be available to the few available to the many. One vivid example of this is entertainment. Until very recently, a music lover would have had to invest thousands of dollars in physical recordings in order to listen to the catalog of music that's now available to stream for anybody with a smartphone. Similarly, online shopping has brought the rarest and most unique specialty items to people living in the most remote parts of the Western world. Democratization is the word for when people of lower means can attain and achieve what was only recently reserved for those with greater means. It should be obvious from this that the internet is one of the greatest democratizing forces in world history, and quite possibly the single greatest.

Democratization, however, has some side-effects. In a 2014 essay that later became a book of the same name, the political commentator Tom Nichols described "the death of expertise," a condition of the internet era in which the free availability of information and the ease with which individuals can express their viewpoint result in an intellectual free-for-all. Nichols writes:

> There was once a time when participation in public debate, even in the pages of the local newspaper, required submission of a letter or an article, and that submission had to be written intelligently, pass editorial review, and stand with the author's name attached. Even then, it was a big deal to get a letter in a major newspaper. Now, anyone can bum rush the comments section of any major publication. Sometimes, that results in a free-for-all that spurs better thinking. Most of the time, however, it means that anyone can post anything they want, under any anonymous cover, and never have to defend their views or get called out for being wrong.[3]

To be sure, the value of "expertise" is often exaggerated by those who have some kind of material interest in being able to refer to themselves as an expert. And a major reason for the weakness of many public institutions and the lack of trust in community leaders has been a pattern of failure and nonresponsibility by those who

---

3 Tom Nichols, "The Death of Expertise," *The Federalist*, January 17, 2014, https://thefederalist .com/.

were appointed "experts." As Nichols acknowledges, experts can get things wrong, and everyone suffers when wrongness is allowed to go unchallenged simply because of where it comes from.

And yet this brings us full circle to a unique dilemma of the internet age. The radical democratization of everything has not only given billions of ordinary people a very real kind of power and voice; it has flattened the distinctions between one voice and another. Offline, a person's advanced degree, years of experience, or endorsement by a respected institution naturally create a distinction between the value of that person's opinion and the value of an average anybody. Further, this distinction—between an expert and a nonexpert—is propped up and reinforced by tangible structures that communicate the expert's qualifications, such as universities, certification boards, and political offices. In other words, in the analog world, society is set up so that while everyone is owed equal justice under the law, not everyone's insights or voices are considered equally valid or worthy of broadcasting.

The web is, in a very real sense, a credential-erasing environment. When everything and everyone is disembodied, these structural distinctions between expert and nonexpert tend to mean very little. What *is* meaningful are *experiences*. Online, personal narratives are the truly authoritative knowledge. Online, it doesn't matter so much who you are, what you've accomplished, or how much you know. What matters is your story. What matters is your truth.

The Power of Story

To illustrate this, let's consider what is unquestionably one of the most revolutionary results of the internet age: the customer review. The centrality of the customer review to the online age is impossible to miss. If you own an iPhone, searching for a restaurant on the Maps application will not only return an establishment's address, hours, and website URL; it will automatically offer a sampling of their latest Yelp reviews. On Amazon the customer star rating is prominently featured under each product name, and you can easily filter your search results by highest rating. Everything on the web is subject to review, and most search engines and landing sites feature these reviews prominently. From therapists to professors, churches to preschools—online, reputation is inseparable from existence. The very *second* people know an institution exists, they can know what others say about it.

The online customer review is a very particular kind of thing. It's almost always written in the first person: "I had this experience at this establishment, and here are my thoughts about it." It's typical for online reviews to blend reaction to the product and to the service into one so that it's not always clear what's being talked about. Most importantly, customer reviews pass evaluative judgments on products, institutions, and even other people that are based foremost on individual experience. Most online reviews use their individual experiences, in many cases only a single experience, to judge the person/product/place, and the experience itself is not open to interpretation, questioning, or pushback. Because it is disembodied like the rest of the internet, the customer review exists absolutely. It can be responded to, it can be disbelieved, but it cannot be challenged in a meaningful way. The individual perspective of the reviewer is isolated from all other considerations.

The online review tells a story, and this story, being one of individual experience, is not an argument that can be debated but a kind of self-expression that is unchallengeable. For example, when looking at reviews of a new local restaurant, you might see a variety of comments about the food, service, or price. But most of these comments will not be worded like scientifically objective evaluations about how well-seasoned the entrees are, or how professionally trained the staff seems, or how the price compares to competitors. Instead, you will see reviews along the lines of, "My steak was cooked well," "The waiters seemed rude and distracted and barely checked on us," or, "The prices are terrible and not worth it." Those comments are more effective in convincing you of something, because they are not just opinions; they are *stories*. And in the online world, your story is your truth.

Of course, this isn't just an internet thing. When Oprah Winfrey said that "speaking your truth is the most powerful tool we all have," she wasn't just thinking about the disembodied web. She was talking about expressive individualism, the notion that being true to oneself, constantly actualizing one's inner desires, perspectives, and feelings, is the epitome of the good life. Nobody needs a smartphone or Twitter account to live according to expressive individualism. It is the ambient worldview of Western culture—the plot to every Disney film, the subtext to every hit song, and the foundation of much of our social and political movements. There's nothing *exclusively* online about it.

And the web is uniquely designed to cultivate expressive individualism in us. It's not just that the internet features millions of articles, influencers, and podcasts that preach expressive individualism directly to our hearts. It's that the *form* of the internet, the very nature of it, serves the centering of the self. Because the web is a radically democratized medium, it is constantly presenting this flattened way of thinking about the world as the desirable norm. When people criticize a historic biblical doctrine by relating a story of how they were treated poorly by someone who believed that doctrine, they are almost certain to be flooded with replies and messages offering support and encouragement for their rejecting that belief. Their post may go viral, being read or watched or shared by thousands of people.

On the other hand, a theologian with decades of experience in reading and teaching Christian doctrine may try to respond with a learned case for not rejecting the doctrine, but he will often be derided as insensitive or even possibly abusive. Responding to a person's story with an argument is, in the world of the web, a fundamental category error. Arguments belong to the world of expertise; stories belong to the world of democratization.

In his essential book *Amusing Ourselves to Death*, Neil Postman made the case that television had recalibrated culture to be more like itself. Postman's primary concern was the trivialization of discourse and excessive entertainment in public life. He saw that more and more experiences in the broader society were becoming less thoughtful, less learned, and more noisy and simplistic. This was happening, Postman believed, because TV had revolutionized how society saw itself:

> Television is our culture's principal mode of knowing about itself. Therefore—and this is the critical point—how television stages the world becomes the model for how the world is properly to be staged. It is not merely that on the television screen entertainment is the metaphor for all discourse. It is that off the screen the same metaphor prevails. As typography once dictated the style of conducting politics, religion, business, education, law, and other important social matters, television now takes command. In courtrooms, classrooms, operating rooms, board rooms, churches and even airplanes, Americans no longer talk

to each other, they entertain each other. They do not exchange ideas; they exchange images.[4]

In other words, according to Postman, as people looked at their TV, they saw lowest-common-denominator language and attention-holding gimmicks. As TV came to dominate their time and attention, eventually they became convinced (even subconsciously) that what they saw there is what the world should look like. Television wasn't simply documenting the world. It was reshaping it.

Perhaps the only thing in Postman's quotation above that has not stood the test of time is the first sentence. Today, it is no longer television that primarily shapes culture. It is the internet. And if trivial entertainment was the decisive ingredient in television that refashioned culture in its image, the parallel ingredient in the World Wide Web is almost certainly the "my story, my truth" ethos.

The social internet is by necessity centered on the self, the user. To go somewhere, you have to choose to click or type. To see something, you have to choose to scroll. Most importantly, to exist in a meaningful way in the online public square, you have to express yourself. You "like" that which interests you. You "share" those things that you enjoy or agree with. The center of gravity in the online world is your profile, in which you are granted a near-godlike ability to craft an identity. Who are you? The answer is whatever your profile says. Your profile picture can be filtered, edited, and adjusted so that you have total control over what everyone else sees when they see "you." No part of your social media life exists apart from your conscious self-disclosure. Unlike in the offline world, when frustrating or embarrassing things often

4 Neil Postman, *Amusing Ourselves to Death* (New York: Penguin, 1985), 92–93.

happen to us in front of others and we are powerless to change what they see, the internet completely collapses the distance between our self-revelation and our identity. We are, and only are, who we choose to be.

This sounds extraordinarily liberating. But a close inspection of the emerging generation of adults who have lived their entire lives under this online catechesis of personal autonomy reveals two important conditions: confusion and exhaustion.

Confusion

It turns out that the radical democratization of everything through the internet is good at doing two things. First, it is good at reducing the amount of confidence that people have in established entities, such as institutions and traditions. This is the analysis of Jonathan Haidt in a widely discussed 2022 cover essay for *The Atlantic* titled, "Why the Past Ten Years of American Life Have Been Uniquely Stupid."[5] Haidt's primary concern is the way that social media has affected political culture. He makes the case that social media platforms encourage us to distrust the processes and networks that tend to safeguard genuine knowledge and productive dialogue. We become self-appointed know-it-alls, eagerly skimming every controversial news story for confirmation bias while we curate feeds that constantly validate us. He concludes that "by rewiring everything in a headlong rush for growth—with a naive conception of human psychology, little understanding of the intricacy of institutions, and no concern for external costs imposed on society—Facebook, Twitter, YouTube, and a few other large platforms unwittingly dissolved the mortar of trust, belief in

---

5   Jonathan Haidt, "Why the Past Ten Years of American Life Have Been Uniquely Stupid," *The Atlantic*, May 2022, https://www.theatlantic.com/.

institutions, and shared stories that had held a large and diverse secular democracy together."[6]

The same point (though with a Christian perspective) is made by theologian Carl R. Trueman. Trueman observes that "for a nation to exist, its members must imagine that they hold things in common that give them a coherent identity as a body of people."[7] This deliberate sense of solidarity, however, can only be undermined as people's individual identities grow more diffuse, and this is precisely the effect that the internet has had:

> If technology in the form of the [birth control] pill helped to undermine traditional sexual codes, then in the form of the internet it helps to weaken the traditional narratives of our imagined communities and offers others to replace them. Indeed, information technology now means that there is a multitude of competing narratives and, consequently, so many different ways of imagining communities. . . . In short, a unified community assumed limited information that allowed for a single dominant narrative to give coherence to the whole.[8]

While these may sound like philosophically interesting but benign observations about the impact of mass information on society, the point here is actually explosive. The internet, especially social media, has untethered scores of people from any solid, given sense of identity or purpose. Recall Nicholas Carr's observation that the web tends to create in us habits of thinking and feeling that align

---

6   Haidt, "Why the Past Ten Years of American Life Have Been Uniquely Stupid."

7   Carl R. Trueman, *Strange New World: How Thinkers and Activists Redefined Identity and Sparked the Sexual Revolution* (Wheaton, IL: Crossway, 2022), 117.

8   Trueman, *Strange New World*, 119.

with its own nature: hypertext, skimming, constant distraction, and maximal input, with no room for careful reflection or givenness. If Neil Postman is correct that technology can not only stage the world but teach us how the world ought to be staged, then it is quite possible that we are becoming the kinds of people who don't even know who we are until we choose to assemble ourselves.

Confusion reigns online. The digital revolution's redistribution of information has led to much public knowledge, but much less public wisdom. With only a phone and a Wi-Fi connection, anyone in the world can access any kind of data, narrative, or argument imaginable. Few, however, would say this has actually led to a culture of widespread expertise. Instead, it foments intense disagreement, especially disagreement wherein people are talking past each other because they have entirely different sources of information. Movements such as #MeToo and #ChurchToo have empowered victims of abuse and mistreatment to force accountability on perpetrators, but they also have relocated the litigation of moral guilt away from institutions of due process onto social media, which can harm victims and accused innocents alike. What's more, the authority that is bestowed on personal narratives creates massive dilemmas for people who want to, as Scripture says, do justice and love mercy (Mic. 6:8). Do we instantly agree with someone's testimony in order to let her know that we care about her and take her life seriously? Do we disregard one person's story entirely on the basis that since we don't have all the facts, we cannot strictly apply a biblical standard of evidence? Do we say and think nothing? Confusion is the order of the day.

Just as the web pushes out of the world of givenness into the world of limitless self-creation, our society is constructing its own meaning out of disparate parts that don't even fit together. There is no higher purpose or meaning to ourselves. There is only more input, more curation, more to add to our "story."

From this vantage point, the transgender revolution not only makes sense; it feels almost inevitable. It must be asked whether the current global despair over defining "man" and "woman" could have ever been possible without the internet. All of the existentialist philosophy in the world could not do for contemporary people the most essential thing to bring about the gender revolution: separate the sense of self from the realm of objective reality. The web, however, can.

The centrality of the disembodied internet to the transgender movement is an inescapable theme of Abigail Shrier's terrifying book *Irreversible Damage: The Transgender Craze Seducing Our Daughters*. Shrier is not a Christian or conservative. She does not believe it is incorrect or unwise for adults to identify as the opposite sex. Yet Shrier believes that the astonishing surge in trans-identifying teen and even preteen girls is not a moment of liberation but one of indoctrination. While her analysis of the trans phenomenon among young girls covers many things other than the internet, social media is clearly one of the most important characters in this narrative. Nearly every case study Shrier describes of a young girl suddenly and totally unexpectedly identifying as a boy includes the girl's immersion into online subcultures that encourage her to identify as trans. The issue was so pervasive that in the book's final chapter, Shrier offers seven pieces of advice to parents to help with the "contagion" of transgender identification, and her number-one warning is, "Don't Get Your Kid a Smartphone."[9] In fact, the power of these technologies to radically affect younger users has

---

9   Abigail Shrier, *Irreversible Damage: The Transgender Craze Seducing Our Daughters* (Washington, DC: Regnery, 2020), 212.

motivated even their inventors to start withholding them from their own children.[10]

The confusion of transgenderism, thus, is really a symptom of a more general confusion about who we are. The logic of gender reassignment is organic to the logic of the internet's self-creation and self-curation. The real "you" is whomever you choose to be seen as. It's not merely that modern people are choosing to consciously reject a transcendent order to their identity. It's that the *idea* of such an order rings intuitively false to a generation of people who have only known themselves via the profile page. It's my story, my truth, because it's my self(ie) and I must decide what it is in the world.

Exhaustion

The second thing that "my story, my truth" is good at is making us very tired. If contemporary culture is marked by claims of absolute liberation and autonomy on the one hand, it is also marked by sadness, loneliness, and exhaustion on the other.

The sociologist Jean Twenge documented the stunning rise in teen anxiety and depression in her 2016 book *iGen*. The book's title refers to the group of Americans born in 1995 or later. In the study, Twenge refers to an "epidemic of anguish" besetting these teens: "56% more teens experienced a major depressive episode in 2015 than in 2010 . . . and 60% more experienced severe impairment."[11] The gap between generations is stark. According to Twenge's research, in 2007 about .8 percent of females ages twelve to fourteen died by suicide. In 2015 the number for the same age

---

10 Nellie Bowles, "Silicon Valley Nannies Are Phone Police for Kids," *New York Times*, October 26, 2018, https://www.nytimes.com/.

11 Jean Twenge, *iGen: Why Today's Super-Connected Kids Are Growing Up Less Rebellious, More Tolerant, Less Happy—and Completely Unprepared for Adulthood* (New York: Atria, 2017), 108.

group was 2.5 percent.[12] Twenge believes her data tells a clear story. "The sudden, sharp rise in depressive symptoms occurred at almost exactly the same time that smartphones became ubiquitous and in-person interaction plummeted."[13]

The reasons for this correlation are hotly debated among social scientists. But Twenge includes a revealing quote from a sixteen-year-old who participated in one of the generational studies. Talking about the pressures of maintaining an online persona, the girl observes, "Every day it's like you have to wake up and put on a mask and try to be somebody else instead of being yourself."[14] Of course, she did not mean this literally. The entire point of social media is for you to be featured on your page, not somebody else. But I think many of us know what she means. Ironically, social media's invitation to "broadcast yourself" has tended to make us feel not more accepted and liked, but less. It turns out that the work of creating ourselves is not energizing but exhausting, even maddening.

Why is this? Consider two reasons. First, the labor of self-creation is founded on the unknowable. If you can find your deepest identity only after it is consciously crafted and curated, the work of crafting and curating runs on zero fuel. Trevin Wax puts it concisely: "People often think that looking into your heart to figure out your desires is the easy part. . . . But that's simply not the case. The truth is, you don't know what will make you happy."[15] Our inability to endlessly know and authenticate ourselves shows up in some small ways in a digital age. Consider what I call "the Netflix Dilemma." Despite

12 Twenge, *iGen*, 111.
13 Twenge, *iGen*, 104.
14 Twenge, *iGen*, 106.
15 Trevin Wax, *Rethink Yourself: The Power of Looking Up Before Looking In* (Nashville, TN: B&H, 2020), 41.

having literally hundreds of options and virtually zero limitation on those options, many people report a feeling of paralysis when trying to figure out what to stream next. The problem is so common that Netflix now offers a "Surprise Me" feature, whereby streamers can avoid having to pick and simply let the service's algorithm make a choice for them. The power of limitless freedom and options does not seem to unleash our creative self-expression as much as it seems to make us wish someone else would think about life on our behalf.

This leads to the second reason creating ourselves exhausts us: it actually doesn't liberate us from the power of another. While the web seems to offer us a way to live above the demands and expectations of our family, church, or community, what we tend to find instead is that it simply repositions us to be submissive to the demands of others. Writer and theologian Alan Noble elegantly describes this condition of modern society, a society that catechizes its members to believe that we only belong to ourselves:

> If we are our own and belong to ourselves, then we are always only who we are. No more. No less. All we have are options and shifting opinions and an overwhelming feeling that whatever the standard might be, we aren't measuring up. Our work is inadequate, our house is inadequate, our tastes are inadequate, our spouse is inadequate, our body is inadequate, our education is inadequate, our cooking is inadequate, and so on. Society cannot fulfill its promise because it never really offered a clear goal. In this sense, the promise of society is more like a warning: You will keep searching, keep expressing, keep redefining, keep striving for your autonomous personhood until you die.[16]

16 Alan Noble, *You Are Not Your Own: Belonging to God in an Inhuman World* (Downers Grove, IL: InterVarsity Press, 2021), 70–71.

Though we may retreat into the safety of self-creation to get out from under some sense of being oppressed, the self-creation actually turns into a form of self-oppression. Without givenness, we have to create the self that we are, and it needs to be a good one if we are to feel validated. How do we know if it is a good one? We check our likes, our comments, our subscribers, our retweets. How do we know if we are speaking the truth? We see how many are agreeing with us. How do we know if we're really living our best life? We try to make it look like those picture-perfect snapshots we see from our favorite influencers. This tireless process of bringing our selves into conformity with a vision of the happy and right wipes us out. We take our revenge on it through periodic breaks. To be happy about ourselves we must occasionally log out of the very same platforms we signed up for in order to be happier about ourselves.

The Alternative

What does it look like to embrace an alternative? If the logic of the web shapes us in the image of expressive individualism, where does Christian wisdom take us?

Christian wisdom tells me that I am not the final authority on myself. I am not self-created or self-sustaining, and therefore I cannot create my own meaning and purpose out of life. What's more, I cannot infallibly interpret even my own experiences. Because I am a creature and not God, it is impossible for me to universalize my desires and intuitions into moral truths.

But the flipside of this is that because I am God's creature, I matter. My story is not absurd or meaningless. There is a transcendent purpose over my life and even my body. Since I cannot create my own meaning, I do not have to. I'm not waiting for society's validation in order to know if I'm being authentic or my best self.

Instead, I can know whether I am living my purpose by finding out whether I am living the way Christ tells me to live.

My story consists of three fundamental realities. First, by choice and by nature, I'm a rebel against my Creator and a cosmic traitor against him. The despair and insecurity of my conscience bear witness that I can't even uphold my own morality perfectly, much less the morality of a holy God. The great church theologian Saint Augustine described sin as a turning from God to self.[17] My nature, my default, is to define reality by the standard of myself, and in this very act I skew toward harming others and myself.

Second, though I am a rebel, I am loved. God in love sent Christ to live the life I should have lived and die the death I deserved to die. Christ lived a perfect story: a beautiful and flawless harmony of utmost love for God and perfect love for his neighbor. Everything Christ did was right, every thought Christ had was pure, every word Christ spoke was true. When he died on the cross, Christ took my sin on himself, absorbing God's wrath against it fully and totally, leaving only Christ's perfect, flawless life, which is now credited to me. This is the greatest act of love that any person could ever do for me, and it has been done for me while I was still a sinner. There is never now a reason to doubt that I matter or have a reason to live, because I am in Christ and Christ is in me.

Finally, the purpose of my life is to experience more deeply the love of Christ for me and to demonstrate this love toward others. I can rejoice with those who rejoice, weep with those who weep, love those who hate me, bless those who curse me, and prefer others even to myself because the love that Christ has poured into my heart gives me the power and desire to be like him. My vocation

---

17 Matt Jenson, *The Gravity of Sin: Augustine, Luther and Barth on* "homo incurvatus in se" (Edinburgh: T&T Clark, 2007), 7.

matters because it is my work to Christ and not just to man, but my vocation does not define me. My relationships matter because Christ has called me to love and serve other people, but my relationships do not define me. My experiences matter because Christ is sovereign over my life and is working all things together for my good, but my experiences do not define me. I don't have to craft an identity or come up with a meaning to my life, because God has called me a son, and in being his son I have and will have everything that Christ has.

That's my story, and I'm sticking to it.

The Abolition of Thought

Digital Liturgy #2: Outrage

NOT LONG AGO I had a strange but enlightening experience. By total chance, a friend and I walked into a small barbecue place for lunch. Sitting near the back I instantly recognized a man with whom I had had some tense social media exchanges. In fact, he had become so frustrated at my beliefs that he blocked me some time ago. No one likes to be blocked, and I was a bit offended when it happened. In any case, I certainly did not expect to run into him, and upon realizing who it was I tried my best not to make eye contact, hopeful that either he would not recognize me or else we would silently agree not to initiate awkward contact.

A few minutes later, something truly odd happened. This man not only saw me, but he got up out of his seat and walked to me and introduced himself. He knew full well who I was, and with perfect politeness he said hello and that it was good to see me. At this point my instinct of southern hospitality took complete control, and I smiled back and exchanged pleasantries. We talked briefly of some mutual friends and what we were up to that day. At no point did anyone mention our (again, contentious) Twitter exchanges, nor did he say anything to the effect of, "I'm sorry I blocked you," or, "Can we talk about our disagreements?" It was like these conversations had never happened.

I soon told a friend who knew this particular man pretty well. Instead of being surprised or confused, my friend just laughed. "That's who this guy is," he said. "He is one way online and a completely different way in person." Later on I couldn't contain my curiosity, so I went back to this man's Twitter page to see if he had perhaps said anything about this encounter. But I was still blocked.

When I talk to friends and others about life in the internet age, stories like this one are perhaps one of the most commonly shared experiences. It seems just about everybody has had some kind of screen-mediated encounter that stressed or even broke a relationship. There's just something about the digital arena that seems to facilitate these unexpected confrontations. A Facebook post about parenting that was meant to be an innocuous observation or encouragement devolves into an emotional argument. A meme or photo that was intended as a joke provokes a heated response. It's very easy online to find yourself in the middle of some kind of dispute before you barely realize it's happening. The entire internet seems combustible.

And once these arguments are happening, how profitable are they? If the romantic vision of the internet is a massive Areopagus, where the common people gather to penetrate mysteries and exchange ideas, the reality of the web is more like a gladiator arena. Despite the democratization of information, despite the close proximity of all of us to oceans of data and arguments inaccessible only decades ago, our online conversations seem to drive us deeper into predug intellectual foxholes. Online debates succeed in making people more convinced that they're right and that the other person is terrible far more often than they succeed in persuading. What's more, often our digital discourse is dead on arrival. "Here are the facts to back up my claim" is met not with concession or careful critique but with, "Oh, yeah? Well here are *my* facts to back up *my* claim." While things like disinformation are certainly major problems in the modern web, when it comes to the hot, flat earth of most social media, what stands out so often is not how much bad information is out there but just how much information at all. As one technology critic put it, "If it feels like people arguing online are living in two different worlds, it's because they are."

And yet, importantly, most of us can't help but notice that the disaster scene we see on our screens is different from the world we experience offline. The fellow who blocked me and then seemed genuinely happy to see me is not as unusual as we might think. In fact, it's a story all too common. All of us seem to inhabit two distinct universes, in which our conversations, our debates, and even our thinking itself seem to undergo some fundamental transformation from the dinner table to the screen. It's not just that the digital world unmasks us, removing our inhibitions and revealing what we're really like. It's as if the digital world helps transform us into something different entirely. To put it simply, it's as if we've all started thinking like the computer algorithms that dominate our day, and in so doing, we've really forgotten how to think.

Meaning and Media

To understand how and why the web has transformed our thinking, we have to carefully consider what thinking online actually looks like.

Nicholas Carr offers a fascinating perspective on the history of reading. The emergence of the book as a worldwide medium was an epistemological revolution, he argues, not least because it demanded (and therefore cultivated) powers of private, concentrated thought and reflection. "Many people had, of course, cultivated a capacity for sustained attention long before the book or even the alphabet came along," Carr writes. "The hunter, the craftsman, the ascetic—all had to train their brains to control and concentrate their attention."[1]

What was so remarkable about book reading was that the deep concentration was combined with the highly active and efficient deciphering of text and interpretation of meaning. The reading of a sequence of printed pages was valuable not just for the knowledge readers acquired from the author's words but for the way those words set off intellectual vibrations within their own minds. In the quiet spaces opened up by the prolonged, undistracted reading of a book, people made their own associations, drew their own inferences and analogies, fostered their own ideas. They thought deeply as they read deeply.[2]

Gutenberg's printing press, Carr notes, was not just a watershed in the history of communication but in the history of thought itself. Because the printing press truly revolutionized the world's access to the linear, analogical experience of individual reading, it resulted in a permanent deepening of cultural thought. "As the book came to be the primary means of exchanging knowledge and insight," Carr notes, "its intellectual ethic became the foundation of our culture."[3] In other words, as the printed page became the

---

1 Nicholas Carr, *The Shallows: What the Internet Is Doing to Our Brains* (New York: Norton, 2010), 64.

2 Carr, *Shallows*, 64.

3 Carr, *Shallows*, 76.

normal means by which ideas were expressed and shared, people's thinking became book-shaped.

Carr is joined in this judgment by Neil Postman. Postman refers to the intellect that is shaped by book reading as the "typographic mind." What stands out about the era of modern history dominated by books, Postman argues, is the greater capacity for expressing real ideas:

> Whenever language is the principal medium of communication—especially language controlled by the rigors of print—an idea, a fact, a claim is the inevitable result. The idea may be banal, the fact irrelevant, the claim false, there is no escape from meaning when language is the instrument guiding one's thought. Though one may accomplish it from time to time, it is very hard to say nothing when employing a written English sentence. What else is exposition good for? Words have very little to recommend them except as carriers of meaning.[4]

A culture that uses printed language to communicate is, according to Postman, a culture of meaning. That meaning may not be true. It could even be absurd. But it *is* meaning. It is comprehensible, communicable, and able to be evaluated. Meaning gives expression shape but also boundaries. The only way you will know if something in this chapter is pure gobbledygook is if you know what meaningful language actually looks like. The typographic mind thinks in a particular way, and that particular way lies at the foundation of much of our society, especially the way we adjudicate our conflicting ideas and beliefs.[5]

---

4   Neil Postman, *Amusing Ourselves to Death* (New York: Penguin, 1985), 50.
5   Interestingly, Postman begins his chapter, "Typographic Mind," with a reflection on the Lincoln-Douglas debates.

For Postman, the dominance of visual media in the twentieth century, especially the television, initiated a new particular way of thought. Postman's chief concern about television was not that it took people away from reading, but that it "re-staged" the world in a trivial way. In other words, by immersing themselves in television, modern people were relearning how to think about themselves, each other, and the world, and the result was a form of thought overwhelmed by shallowness and titillation. "But what I am claiming here is not that television is entertaining but that it has made entertainment itself the natural format for all representation of all experience."[6] Postman's primary target for this critique was television news, which imposed a form of mindless entertainment (via quick cuts, jingly music, the "banter" of the newscasters, etc.) on even matters of life and death. The net effect of TV's transformation on public discourse was not simply to make the daily headlines more frivolous, but to recalibrate the public's attitude toward the world itself: to always expect frivolity and resist sobriety, to need noise and flee from silence. Minds that were fixated on how TV staged the world started to create a world that felt more like TV.

This, finally, brings us back full circle to the web. Just as Postman observed that the rules of the medium of television transformed the way a TV society speaks, so Nicholas Carr observes that the rules of the internet and the digital medium are likewise changing the way an internet society thinks. We looked at some of these effects in chapter 3, but we stopped short of connecting them to the wider decay of thought we can observe online.

Carr makes the case that the kind of thinking we do when engaging with a book or other printed language is qualitatively different

6 Postman, *Amusing Ourselves to Death*, 87.

from the kind of thinking we do when we are reading online. Just as TV has certain rules that make it tend toward the frivolous and entertaining, the web has certain rules that make it tend toward the diffuse and distracting. But it also has a rule that pushes us away from slow and careful reflection and toward a kind of zombie-like pursuit of the next neurological reward:

> The Net also provides a high-speed system for delivering re-sponses and rewards— "positive reinforcements," in psychologi-cal terms—which encourage the repetition of both physical and mental actions. When we click a link, we get something new to look at and evaluate. When we Google a keyword, we receive, in the blink of an eye, a list of interesting information to ap-praise. When we send a text or an instant message or an email, we often get a reply in a matter of seconds or minutes. When we use Facebook, we attract new friends or form closer bonds with old ones. When we send a tweet through Twitter, we gain new followers. When we write a blog post, we get comments from readers or links from other bloggers.[7]

Here, Carr makes a vital observation. In the offline world, the experience of reading and reflecting is often siloed away from these other kinds of experiences. When we open a book, we don't automatically send a notification to our friends about what we're reading. When we're thinking hard about a particular argument, we're not getting a hit of dopamine from the appearance of a new notification. In the analog world, our intellectual and social experi-ences, while certainly working together, are not *bound up* with each

---

7   Carr, *Shallows*, 117.

other. This separation is crucial to cultivating wisdom, because there will always be social reasons to think foolishly or poorly.

Believing and Belonging

In the opening chapter of C. S. Lewis's *The Screwtape Letters*, the demon Screwtape is advising his nephew and protégé, Wormwood, on how to keep a human (the demon's "patient") from getting serious about the claims of Christianity (the "Enemy"). Screwtape encourages Wormwood to keep the patient away from any kind of rational consideration about religion and to instead focus his attention on whether religion is the kind of thing that he should *want* to be true:

> Your man has been accustomed, ever since he was a boy, to have a dozen incompatible philosophies dancing about together inside his head. He doesn't think of doctrines as primarily "true" or "false," but as "academic" or "practical," "outworn" or "contemporary," "conventional" or "ruthless." Jargon, not argument, is your best ally in keeping him from the Church. Don't waste time trying to make him think that materialism is *true*! Make him think it is strong, or stark, or courageous—that it is the philosophy of the future. That is the sort of thing he cares about. The trouble about argument is that it moves the whole struggle on to the Enemy's own ground.[8]

Lewis believed, rightly, that there was a difference between a genuine, diligent search for the truth and thinking in jargon. Jargon is what happens when the desire to be seen as a certain kind of person outweighs the desire to know what's real. Jargon is what

8 C. S. Lewis, *The Screwtape Letters* (New York: HarperCollins, 1942), 1–2.

happens when the search for facts and ultimate reality gives way to a thirst for validation. To think in jargon is not to ask, *Is this true?* but, *How will believing this reflect on me to others?*

Certainly it is normal and healthy to desire love and respect from others. And there is absolutely a social element in our pursuit of truth. This is why so much of the Bible both depicts and commands membership in a spiritual community, united by the gospel and knit together through the work of the Spirit. But there is a profound difference between thinking in community toward the true, the good, and the beautiful, and outsourcing that thinking to the crowd. The former creates thinkers who are steadfast, consistent, humbled, and eager for others to join on the journey. The latter creates jargon flingers who are volatile, inconsistent, proud, and so dependent on their special status as a member of the in-group that in a very real sense, they really don't want others to agree with them. Their status as enlightened ones must be preserved.

All it takes is a few minutes logged into social media to see a live conflict between good thinking and jargon-addled social posturing. I'm not talking about conflict between one person or group and another. I'm talking about a conflict inside all of us. To be on seemingly any social media at all is to regularly experience intellectual and emotional fatigue. Do I respond to that one person's erroneous post? Should I intervene in this argument between people on my feed? What should I do with this article or video or meme sent to me? Even seemingly innocuous announcements are potential landmines. If you want to make people angry online, talk about politics or religion. If you want to make people furious, talk about parenting.

The point I'm getting at is that there's a reason that thinking online is so perilous. The internet is an epistemological habitat that makes genuine wisdom difficult and unappealing. The web makes it easy and rewarding to engage in knee-jerk judgments, emotivism, and fallacies. Further, this is not an accident. The social internet is designed for one purpose: to keep us scrolling, keep us posting, keep us hooked. Negative emotions—feelings of anger, frustration, or disagreement—are to social media scrolling what coal is to a steam locomotive. In a revealing interview, Tristan Harris, a former Google engineer who has become a strident critic of social media's effect on culture, explains how these algorithms are designed to overwhelm users with a certain kind of feeling:

> Outrage just spreads faster than something that's not outrage.
>
> When you open up the blue Facebook icon, you're activating the AI, which tries to figure out the perfect thing it can show you that'll engage you. It doesn't have any intelligence, except figuring out what gets the most clicks. The outrage stuff gets the most clicks, so it puts that at the top.
>
> Then it learns there's this magic keyword where if any article had this keyword and you put it at the top of the feed, it would always get a click or a share. And that keyword was "Trump." If you're just a naive computer, you put this keyword in front of people and they always click it. It's reinforcing that this is the thing that should go to the top of the feed.[9]

Harris then asks, "What does seeing a repeated set of things that make you outraged do to you?"

> You can feel it when it happens. I think of it as civilization mind control. It's not that there's someone who's deliberately trying

---

9 Ezra Klein, "How Technology Is Designed to Bring Out the Worst in Us," *Vox*, rev. February 19, 2018, https://www.vox.com/.

to make us all outraged. It's that 2 billion people, from the moment they wake up in the morning, are basically jacked into an environment, where if you're a teenager, the first thing you see are photo after photo of your friends having fun without you. That does something to all those human animals. If the first thing you do when your eyes open is see Twitter and there's a bunch of stuff to be outraged about, that's going to do something to you on an animal level.

I think what we have to reckon with is how this is affecting us on a deeper level.[10]

Harris's insights are disturbing and illuminating. But like the majority of cultural critics, Harris does not express a true north for good thinking. Harris is chiefly concerned about the manipulation of human behavior by Big Tech, but he stops well short of articulating a true moral case against it. Likewise, many other recent books that reflect on the epistemological habitat of the web offer surprisingly few answers. Concerns about "misinformation," outrage culture, and polarization are frequently unaccompanied by any presentation of what real wisdom looks like or an alternative way to think that is more true, more humane, and more just.[11]

Three Characteristics of Christian Thinking

To think as a Christian means that knowing something is off isn't enough. Christian wisdom is not a texture-less posture of pure critique. Rather, it is a gospel-shaped, Spirit-empowered intellectual

---

10 Klein, "How Technology Is Designed to Bring Out the Worst in Us."

11 I expanded on this point in a review of *The Constitution of Knowledge* by Jonathan Rauch: Samuel James, "My Facts Versus Your Facts: Can We Really Know Truth?" The Gospel Coalition, January 27, 2022, https://www.thegospelcoalition.org/.

habit that reflects spiritual reality. It would be beyond the ability of this author to try to articulate a Christian way to think about every pressing theological, social, or personal issue (and it would certainly be beyond the accepted page count of a single book!). So instead of offering a line item of "stuff Christians should believe about *X*," I'd like to end this chapter by reflecting on three distinctive characteristics of Christian thinking.

Before we do that, I want to offer two preliminary cautions. First, these characteristics are rooted in Scripture's revelation of who God is and what he wants his people to think. These are not, however, "strategies" that will make Christians more convincing or persuasive when arguing with others. Particularly regarding the topics of technology and social media, it's easy to think about Christian wisdom as a helpful "middle way" that will enable winsome believers to fly above the culture wars. I'm not sure such a thing is even desirable. But I am sure that such a thing is mere fantasy. It is not only possible to think well and Christianly and still end up ignored, rejected, or even persecuted; it is, according to Jesus, *inevitable* (John 16:2). When we seek to think well as Christians, we do so because we believe it will lead us to genuine truth. As C. S. Lewis pointed out, "If Christianity is untrue, then no honest man will want to believe it, however helpful it might be: if it is true, every honest man will want to believe it, even if it gives him no help at all."[12]

Second, these characteristics work with one another rather than against each other. By that I mean that it's a mistake to take any one of these characteristics and set it up as the chief standard that governs all others. Christian thinking is careful, but it is not so careful that it avoids deep community. Christian thinking is calm,

---

12 C. S. Lewis, "Man or Rabbit," in *God in the Dock* (Grand Rapids, MI: Eerdmans, 1970), 109.

but it does not use calmness as an excuse to not confidently tell the truth. Many of the pitfalls we fall into as Christians are there simply because we try (even unwittingly) to pit one truth against another.

So with those cautions in hand, what are three characteristics of genuinely Christian thinking?

1. Christian thinking is careful.

We saw earlier that one of the hallmarks of digital thinking is that it relies on intuition and makes snap judgments. Christian thinking is different. Rather than drawing quick conclusions, Christian thinking seeks out the other half of the story. "The one who states his case first seems right, until the other comes and examines him" (Prov. 18:17). Contrary to the ethos of the web, where beating others to the punch and getting an opinion out there quickly are keys to success, genuine insight is possible only with deliberate restraint. "Be not rash with your mouth, nor let your heart be hasty to utter a word before God, for God is in heaven and you are on earth. Therefore let your words be few" (Eccl. 5:2). Christian carefulness does not come out of a place of timidity or confusion. Rather, it stems from a deep awareness of the powerful intellectual effects of the fall and the reality-distorting power of the world, the flesh, and the devil. Judging by outward appearances tends to be useful in confirming what we already believed to be true, but it is not how God looks at the world (1 Sam. 16:7).

One of the great challenges to careful Christian thinking, particularly online, is anger. Anger is a powerful epistemological fog. Anger—at those with the wrong views, at those who attack us, sometimes just at those who don't go about things the way we do—wrecks Christian thinking. No wonder the Bible gives us warning after warning about anger. "Refrain from anger, and forsake wrath!"

(Ps. 37:8). Social media's algorithmic design to elicit our anger so as to command our attention is nothing less than a moral crisis.

Those who quickly point out that anger can sometimes be righteous and that Jesus himself demonstrated some anger are missing the point. The overwhelming normative pattern for the people of God is to resist anger. "Know this, my beloved brothers: let every person be quick to hear, slow to speak, slow to anger; for the anger of man does not produce the righteousness of God" (James 1:19–20). While there are times and occasions for a holy anger, our social media–immersed age is one in which for every individual who needs an infusion of hot-blooded zeal, there are probably a hundred others slowly combusting under the emotional and spiritual pressure of pointless, graceless, nonredemptive anger.

Given the spiritual content of anger, and given the connection between anger and foolish, unreal thinking, one of the most important things Christians can do in the public square is to live and talk and post in such a way that demonstrates a calm confidence in the sovereignty of Jesus. Righteous people can become angry. Angry people have a very hard time being righteous. But the more convinced we are of the power and total truthfulness of God's word, the less volatile we will be when our beliefs and values are challenged. For those who have only earthly citizenship, every argument, every challenge, every debate is a potential threat to their identity and security. Those with a heavenly city, however, are free to be calm, free to be silent, free to reflect carefully, because they know their fate is sealed.

2. Christian thinking is truthful.

"Duh," you might think! It's not exactly a scorching hot take to say that Christian thinking cares about truth. But what's less obvious are the ways, especially in the digital era, that the Christian pursuit of truth can be undermined. To say that genuinely Christian thinking is truthful may not seem like a radical thing, but putting this into practice in the world of the web requires radical practices indeed.

Earlier, we observed that one of the intrinsic challenges that the internet poses to clear, precise thinking is the way it bundles the social with the intellectual. The web, by "collapsing" categories of human thought into one flat medium, pushes away from deep, personal reflection and toward the neural rewards of the notification and the Like button. Interestingly, an encounter between Jesus and some Jews expresses very similar themes. In John 5, Jesus performs an astonishing miracle of healing for a man who had been unable to walk for nearly forty years. With nothing more than his words, Jesus instantly reverses decades of disease and muscular atrophy, and the man—previously not even able to crawl into a nearby pool—picks up his bed and walks.

Now, a rational response to this amazing display of both divine power and tender compassion would have been to fall at Jesus's feet. But this particular group of Jews is not thinking rationally. Instead of wanting to follow and worship Jesus, they want to kill him (v. 18), because he claims to be equal with God and chooses to break their customs by healing on the Sabbath. In an ensuing exchange, Jesus makes a surprising and crucial insight into the motivations of his accusers:

I have come in my Father's name, and you do not receive me. If another comes in his own name, you will receive him. How can you believe, when you receive glory from one another and do not seek the glory that comes from the only God? (John 5:43–44)

Jesus could have attributed the unbelief of this group to many things: jealousy over his influence, resentment of his power, even simple ignorance. Instead, Christ says that their coming to him in faith is prevented by the fact that they receive glory from each other. In other words, there is something about the way this group affirms and puffs each other up that actively stops them from seeing Jesus for who he is.

Glory from others is a powerful reality distorter, and in the age of social media, it is one of the most profound threats to truthful Christian thinking. When the act of thinking is inseparable from the act of being noticed, approved, or shared, the threat of thinking *for the sake of those things* is omnipresent. It is evident in the way we feel we must pipe in on the latest controversy, often posting and then anxiously awaiting the little chimes of affirmation that simultaneously reinforce our opinion and our desire for additional validation. It is evident in the way we tend to ask not whether such and such argument is really true or verifiable but whether the right kind of people ("our" kind of people) believe it or not. It is evident in the way we assume that because a person took a position we disagreed with in the past, he or she is probably not trustworthy on this new topic. The Jews to whom Jesus spoke were letting their egos think for them, and their egos did not want them to see the truth.

In a 1944 lecture, C. S. Lewis warned a roomful of young men about the intellectual and moral pitfalls of an insatiable desire to belong. "The Inner Ring" remains, in my view, one of Lewis's best and most insightful pieces. A solid sixty years before anybody would utter the words "social media," Lewis sketched out the dangers of letting desires for social approval drive belief. "In the whole of your life as you now remember it," Lewis asks his audience, "has the desire to be on the right side of that invisible line ever prompted you to any act or word on which, in the cold small hours of a wakeful night, you can look back with satisfaction? If so, your case is more fortunate than most." He continues:

> My main purpose in this address is simply to convince you that this desire is one of the great permanent mainsprings of human action. It is one of the factors which go to make up the world as we know it—this whole pell-mell of struggle, competition, confusion, graft, disappointment and advertisement, and if it is one of the permanent mainsprings then you may be quite sure of this. Unless you take measures to prevent it, this desire is going to be one of the chief motives of your life, from the first day on which you enter your profession until the day when you are too old to care. . . . If you do nothing about it, if you drift with the stream, you will in fact be an "inner ringer." I don't say you'll be a successful one; that's as may be. But whether by pining and moping outside Rings that you can never enter, or by passing triumphantly further and further in—one way or the other you will be that kind of man.[13]

"Of all the passions," Lewis concludes, "the passion for the Inner Ring is most skillful in making a man who is not yet a very bad man do very bad things."[14] To which we would only add: it is most skillful in making someone who is not yet a bad thinker become a bad thinker.

The commitment to Christian thinking is not a total rejection of having a "tribe" (as we'll see in a moment). It is, however, a

---

13 C. S. Lewis, "The Inner Ring," in *The Weight of Glory and Other Addresses* (New York: HarperCollins, 1941), 151–52.
14 Lewis, "Inner Ring," 154.

rejection of tribe worship. The fact that people share your convictions about some things does not make them automatically right about others, and the reverse is also true: those with whom we sharply disagree on major questions can still tell the truth, and we fail morally when we fail to listen to the truth simply because of where it comes from. Just as Paul did not assume that his fellow apostle Peter was correct to withdraw from the Gentiles (Gal. 2:11), just as Rehoboam forever devastated Israel's kingdom because he listened uncritically to his buddies (1 Kings 12), we have an obligation to not let our lists of friends and enemies dictate what we will believe. Likes and shares are not measures of truthfulness; accordance with God's word is. A person's political affiliation or theological membership does not dictate his ability to say true things. We can maintain vital worldview distinctions while also believing that God wants us to think things that are true, even things that might challenge our tribe or cause us to reexamine our assumptions.

3. Christian thinking is communal.

If "inner-ringism" is a threat on one side of the internet age, the threat on the far side might be called "lone-rangerism." The web's disembodied character powerfully distorts our perception of reality. Isolated in the presence of the screen, we become more and more turned in on ourselves. In a way, this effect of the web is what inflames all others. Left to ourselves, we don't sense when our anger and anxiety are clouding our wisdom. Left to ourselves, we can't see our slide into unthinking partisanship. The Bible is not naive about our struggle to think wisely and Christianly. God knows we are like grass. Precisely because of that, Scripture directs Christians to the heart-shaping habitat of the local church, where, through the power of the liturgy and the presence of Christ's Spirit in his people, we are formed more closely in the image of Jesus.

Not long ago I read a discussion online about whether "civility" was really a virtue we should pursue. While there were some insightful questions about how injustice might be hidden behind norms of discourse, I came away from the conversation with the unshakable sense that this was a very internet thing to talk about. On the computer, "civility" may be a mere abstraction, a philosophical principle that can be interrogated and perhaps jettisoned. But offline, in the physical world of work, family, church, and neighborhood, "civility" is simply what's required to live among other people. Offline, if you open the door to someone else's house, enter her living room, and start yelling at her, you may be arrested, and few people would feel sorry for you. But on the internet, starting arguments with total strangers, for no apparent reason, is normal. In fact, we almost expect it. It's nearly impossible to overstate how fundamentally the disembodied nature of the web has recalibrated our sense of what is good and normal.

Christian thinking pursues embodied community. Before physical people, with human faces we can read, human voices in which we can hear emotion, saying human words that bind us emotionally to a particular place and a particular moment, we are reminded of what the Bible really means by honoring one another, serving one another, preferring one another, loving one another, admonishing one another, confessing your sins to one another, and praying for one another. Pixels are not created in God's image. People are. It is a holy thing to be with another human being. It is, in fact, our eternal destiny.

Throughout secular culture, places of in-person gathering and embodied relationships are in decline. Jobs have gone remote.

Streaming has crippled the cinema and concert industries. Classrooms are virtual, support groups are digital, and even dating is now centered around apps. In many communities, churches are some of the only physical centers of human gathering left. This is neither accidental nor arbitrary. Christianity does not reduce the self to the screen-mediated mind. We belong, as the catechism says, body and soul, to God. Our pursuit of the truth must take us nearer to other people and physical life, not away from it.

Renewal

"Do not be conformed to this world," Paul writes, "but be transformed by the renewal of your mind, that by testing you may discern what is the will of God, what is good and acceptable and perfect" (Rom. 12:2). God is not content to renew our consciences. He wants us to be renewed in our minds, a renewal that transforms us to look unlike the world—in all its angst, foolishness, and unreality—and pushes us toward what is good and acceptable and perfect. What is the outworking of this mind renewal? Paul tells us:

> For by the grace given to me I say to everyone among you not to think of himself more highly than he ought to think, but to think with sober judgment, each according to the measure of faith that God has assigned. For as in one body we have many members, and the members do not all have the same function, so we, though many, are one body in Christ, and individually members one of another. (Rom. 12:3–5)

Humility. Sober judgment. Faith. In view of what? In view of other people, other "members" in "one body," part of Christ and part of each other. A renewal of the mind is not simply a worldview course correction. It's not primarily a new idea. It's not even ultimately about technology. It's about a deep and abiding habit of careful, calm, truthful, and communal thinking, expressing itself in faith and testing and all that is perfect. This is the kind of thinking that can cut through any fog, even digital. This is the kind of thinking that bears witness to the divine Logos and results in flourishing bearers of the Logos's image. This is the kind of thinking that we will never regret.

6

Shame on You

Digital Liturgy #3: Shame

IN 2010 HELEN RITTELMEYER was a journalist working in the Washington, DC, area. That October, an exciting opportunity came her way: she would appear on C-SPAN as part of a panel discussion on the future of American conservatism. Also appearing on the same panel would be a fellow journalist named Todd Seavey, who just happened to be Helen's ex-boyfriend. If the C-SPAN panel presented at first like an opportunity for some right-of-center writers to thoughtfully reflect on ideas in a format that could benefit their respective careers, for Helen, it soon turned into a living nightmare.

In response to a question, Seavey, with cameras rolling, started to berate Helen personally. What had been a seemingly political discussion quickly became humiliation, as Seavey criticized Helen as a bad thinker, a bad girlfriend, even a bad person. "For three minutes and forty-five seconds, which, unfortunately for me, were captured on film for broadcast two weeks later on C-SPAN2,"

Helen would reflect, "he made an impassioned case that I was a sociopath."[1]

Those three minutes and forty-five seconds would prove to be significant in Helen's (now Helen Andrews) life. Writing about this chapter in her life nearly a decade later, Helen recalled that the clip immediately went viral, triggering a deluge of reaction and commentary around the internet, some of which was supportive and much of which was not. "My colleagues probably didn't believe the woman they worked alongside was secretly a comic-book villain—but surely the suspicion had been planted," she writes. "I never knew whether someone on the subway was giving me a second glance because he knew me, or because he recognized me from the video."

According to Helen, the clip followed her nearly everywhere she went: in job interviews, meetings with students, even eight years after the panel when someone tried to show the clip (unknowingly) to Helen's husband. She revisited the episode as part of an essay on the epidemic of online shaming. "The more online shame cycles you observe," she writes, "the more obvious the pattern becomes: Everyone comes up with a principled-sounding pretext that serves as a barrier against admitting to themselves that, in fact, all they have really done is joined a mob. Once that barrier is erected, all rules of decency go out the window, but the pretext is almost always a lie."[2]

People who have been at the center of an online humiliation campaign learn, she argues, that the only possible response is to endure it. The internet's ambient omnipresence in every facet of culture makes any attempt to control or push back against online

---

1   Helen Andrews, "Shame Storm," *First Things*, January 2019, https://www.firstthings.com/.
2   Andrews, "Shame Storm."

mobs hopeless. In some cases the target of the mob really has done something objectionable (such as insult or mistreat someone), but in the vast majority of those cases the response of the online mob becomes wildly disproportionate to the actual crime. More often, however, the people in a shame storm have not really done anything wrong. Instead, they've become a symbol for something else, something ancient: the urgent need for a culture to have something, or someone, to absorb their indwelling sense of sin.

The New Scaffolds

In the April 1886 issue of *The Atlantic Monthly* Julian Hawthorne, son of Nathaniel, reviewed his father's novel *The Scarlet Letter*. In the novel, a young woman named Hester Prynne is branded by her community with a red *A* due to her giving birth out of wedlock. Nathaniel Hawthorne's novel deconstructs moral hypocrisy by revealing that it is the town's revered minister, Arthur Dimmesdale, who is the father of Hester's child. Toward the conclusion of his over-nine-thousand-word essay, Julian Hawthorne reflected on the irony of the book's moralistic context:

> This [the scarlet *A*] is her punishment, the heaviest that man can afflict upon her. But, like all legal punishment, it aims much more at the protection of society than at the reformation of the culprit. Hester is to stand as a warning to others tempted as she was: if she recovers her own salvation in the process, so much the better for her; but, for better or worse, society has ceased to have any concern with her.
>
> "We trample you down," society says in effect to those who break its laws, "not by any means in order to save your soul,—for the welfare of that problematical adjunct to your civic personality

is a matter of complete indifference to us,—but because, by some act, you have forfeited your claim to our protection, because you are a clog to our prosperity, and because the spectacle of your agony may discourage others of similar unlawful inclinations."

But it is obvious, all the while, that the only crime which society recognizes is the crime of being found out, since a society composed of successful hypocrites would much more smoothly fulfill all social requirements than a society of such heterogeneous constituents as (human nature being what it is) necessarily enter into it now.[3]

The idea of a world that encourages moral hypocrisy through punitive shaming is often associated, thanks in no small part to *The Scarlet Letter*, with religion. But the contemporary West demonstrates a fascinating paradox. As the importance of religion has decreased and expressive individualism has increased, the result has not been a culture-wide renewal of compassion, tolerance, and understanding. Instead, the social internet has documented an astonishingly ascendant shame culture that digitally punishes and erases those who run afoul of its values. There are different names for this phenomenon such as cancel culture, online mobs, and shame storms. But they all describe something that nearly everyone who spends meaningful time on social media has witnessed at one point or another. Despite the alleged democratizing effects of the web, modern online adults seem remarkably powerless before their own screen. A tasteless joke, a wrongly timed opinion, a thoughtless remark: all of these and much more are sufficient to brand people online in a way that can genuinely alter their life.

3 Julian Hawthorne, "'The Scarlet Letter,' by Nathaniel Hawthorne, Reviewed," *The Atlantic Monthly*, April 1886, https://www.theatlantic.com/.

While many instances of online cancellation feature relatively high-profile personalities, the moral logic and progression of shame culture can affect anyone. Jon Ronson's landmark book *So You've Been Publicly Shamed* is a compendium of stories of those who have suffered career or relational losses because of an online shame storm. In *The Coddling of the American Mind*, Jonathan Haidt and Greg Lukianoff chronicle the regression of free speech and debate in education and the rise of "witch hunts," often featuring groups of online students or activists who pressure those with unwanted opinions out of the public eye.[4] The perception that cancel culture is merely a conceptual mirage that affects only certain kinds of journalists or celebrities is mistaken. Among ordinary people, friendship across political and social divides is diminishing, as fewer people in the West (especially fewer Americans) are willing to befriend and live with those with opposing viewpoints.[5] This decline is itself a soft form of "cancel culture," one that may avoid public spectacle but still follows the logic of tearing down whatever is challenging or uncomfortable.

It was not very long ago that many Christians believed we were living in an age of unfettered relativism. "That's true for you, and this is true for me" was supposedly the indefatigable orthodoxy of the postmodern West. Its philosophy is illustrated in a scene from *Indiana Jones and the Last Crusade*, where the legendary archaeologist is teaching his university class that "archaeology is the search for facts, not truth. If it's truth you're interested in, Dr. Tyree's

---

4 Jonathan Haidt and Greg Lukianoff, *The Coddling of the American Mind: How Good Intentions and Bad Ideas Are Setting Up a Generation for Failure* (New York: Penguin, 2018), 99–121.

5 Linley Sanders, "Americans Are Less Likely to Have Friends of Very Different Political Opinions Compared to 2016," YouGov America, October 6, 2020, https://today.yougov .com/.

Philosophy class is right down the hall."[6] The contrast of "truth" as an ephemeral abstraction versus "fact" as objective reality summarizes well the spirit of relativism. But in the last few years, this mentality has evaporated. Activism for the sake of racial justice or #MeToo has illustrated that the emerging generation of Western adults does not, in fact, think "what works for you, works for you." Instead, the moral claims of justice have reshaped society so that to oppose what is perceived as justice is not an acceptable expression of individual morality but an offense against culture. Moral relativism is dead, and the hashtag helped kill it.

What explains this seemingly contradictory decline of religion and rise of (secular) moral absolutism? One answer may be found in the religious decline itself. Summarizing philosopher Charles Taylor's analysis of modernity and the "buffered self" that feels no closeness to things spiritual or transcendent, Christian pastor and writer John Starke observes that this loss of religious presupposition leads to a cultural feeling of meaninglessness:

> It is what Taylor calls a sense of "malaise," which senses the world to be a flat, empty place, where what we've gained with our buffered selves doesn't compensate for what we've lost with transcendence. The malaise deepens because even though we have given up on transcendent reality, we haven't given up on transcendent feelings and experiences. We instead look for transcendence within an immanent frame, which only exposes the smallness of our reality and intensifies the sense of loss.[7]

---

6 *Indiana Jones and the Last Crusade*, directed by Steven Spielberg (Hollywood, CA: Paramount Pictures, 1989).

7 John Starke, "Preaching to the Secular Age," in *Our Secular Age: Ten Years of Reading and Applying Charles Taylor*, ed. Collin Hansen (Deerfield, IL: The Gospel Coalition, 2017), 44.

One way to understand the emergence of online shaming and the encouragement of estrangement from those deemed "enemy" is as a kind of numbing agent for the malaise that Starke (and Taylor) describe here. The loss of definitive moral categories across the West, particularly in spaces of higher education, did not liberate modern people from fear and guilt. But it did train them to believe that such things are illegitimate, that they signify nothing of existential value, and that the only way to deal with them is to not. It is impossible for human beings to function this way, because, regardless of whatever ideologies we internalize, we remain created in the image of God—unable to totally buffer ourselves from the sense that there is indeed something greater than us outside of us, and that our access to that greatness is hindered by something within us. The question is not whether we will sense this, for we certainly will. The question is, given this sensation, and given the erasure of the moral categories to deal with it, what will we do?

Why Sin and Shame Won't Go Away

This question serves as the setting for one of the most important essays I've read in the past several years. In "The Strange Persistence of Guilt," scholar Wilfred McClay considers two competing cultural trends. First, there is the overwhelming psychologization of guilt and shame. Few ideas enjoy such uniformity of consensus among elite educators as the idea that any sense of moral failing or despair at one's flaws must be reinterpreted in therapeutic terms. You are *not* guilty. You are simply held to oppressive standards by your community (especially your family). Your shame tells you nothing except that you need to actualize your authentic self and be and do whatever your heart tells you.

Second, however, McClay observes that despite such therapeutic answers to guilt and shame, modern people do not appear more at peace or more reconciled with themselves. Instead, contemporary culture is brimming with unrest, anxiety, and, yes, even a profound kind of guilt. Under the influence of thinkers such as Sigmund Freud, modern people now believe their indwelling sense of shame is an ailment that must be massaged or cured. But since their feelings cannot really go away, the suppressed sense of moral guilt must go *somewhere*. McClay considers the fact that this suppressed shame appears to be going in the direction of other people:

The presence of vast amounts of unacknowledged sin in a culture, a culture full to the brim with its own hubristic sense of world-conquering power and agency but lacking any effectual means of achieving redemption for all the unacknowledged sin that accompanies such power: This is surely a moral crisis in the making—a kind of moral-transactional analogue to the debt crisis that threatens the world's fiscal and monetary health. The rituals of scapegoating, of public humiliation and shaming, of multiplying morally impermissible utterances and sentiments and punishing them with disproportionate severity, are visibly on the increase in our public life. They are not merely signs of intolerance or incivility, but of a deeper moral disorder, an *Unbehagen* that cannot be willed away by the psychoanalytic trick of pretending that it does not exist.[8]

McClay points out that Christianity offers sinners genuine forgiveness precisely because it executes an atonement that si-

8   Wilfred McClay, "The Strange Persistence of Guilt," *Hedgehog Review* 19 (Spring 2017), https://hedgehogreview.com/.

multaneously confirms the realness of guilt, satisfies justice, and liberates the sinner. Thus, every part of the human person (and human culture) that is affected by this sense of guilt and shame is sufficiently accounted for. Our guilt is not illusory, but we are not hopelessly obliterated by it because in grace it is transferred to someone who possesses both the authority and the willingness to bear it on our behalf.

But what happens at a cultural level when this story disappears from a society's consciousness? The answer, according to McClay, is that our quest for some kind of moral assurance finds scapegoats elsewhere. McClay points out that some people navigate this world by trying to become victims to whom society owes a sacrifice. Others, however, respond by slaking their consciences by sacrificing others for their sin. McClay concludes that this is a dilemma that a secular age cannot solve:

> Science cannot do anything to relieve the guilt weighing down our souls, a weight to which it has added appreciably, precisely by rendering us able to be in control of, and therefore accountable for, more and more elements in our lives—responsibility being the fertile seedbed of guilt. That growing weight seeks opportunities for release, seeks transactional outlets, but finds no obvious or straightforward ones in the secular dispensation. Instead, more often than not we are left to flail about, seeking some semblance of absolution in an incoherent post-Christian moral economy that has not entirely abandoned the concept of sin but lacks the transactional power of absolution or expiation without which no moral system can be bearable.[9]

9 McClay, "The Strange Persistence of Guilt."

The unbearable quality of our atonement-less public religion is on vivid display in the social media age. Despite the triumph of the strange new world of identity politics and sexual revolution, we in the contemporary West have not been able to eliminate our moralistic instincts. Rather, we instead discharge them under a new moral code, one that tends to replace deity with abstractions such as justice and equality, redefine sin as pure bigotry, and offer no mechanism for atonement but only a ritual by which the religious community can purge themselves of those who bring dishonor on it.

Jean Twenge's book *iGen* captures this new cultural moment statistically. Consider two parallel truths about emerging American adults: they are abandoning religious affiliation (in record numbers) because religion is (they say) too intolerant of LGBT people; *and* they are more likely than any other American generation before them to demand from their school, their employer, or their community protection from ideas and opinions they dislike. According to Twenge's research, the percentage of first-year college students who affiliated with a religion sat at 85 percent in 1998. In 2016 that number was 68 percent and trending further downward.[10] Twenge writes, "More young people now associate religion with rigidity and intolerance—an automatic anathema to a highly individualistic and accepting generation."[11]

And yet when the topic turns to politics instead of religion, individualism and acceptance give way to a desire for conformity. Twenge lists several incidents involving young college students who

---

10 Jean Twenge, *iGen: Why Today's Super-Connected Kids Are Growing Up Less Rebellious, More Tolerant, Less Happy—and Completely Unprepared for Adulthood* (New York: Atria, 2017), 122.

11 Twenge, *iGen*, 139.

supported someone's firing or academic suspension for voicing the wrong opinion. "What's changed recently," Twenge observes, "is that more and more statements are deemed racist or sexist and more and more speakers are deemed 'extreme.'"[12] Whereas students decry organized religion for its rules and exclusions, they are much more comfortable than their parents with demanding that ideas and people that upset them go away. The alternative to traditional religion has not proved to be a radically egalitarian society made up of autonomous individuals allowed to define their own reality. Rather, the alternative is simply a new moral code, but one that is more fluid, less predictable, and beholden to the values of public relations and the-customer-is-always-right. Morality, guilt, and punishment have not disappeared. They're just under new management.

Repentance and Grace in a Callout Culture

Of all the different digital liturgies discussed in this book, it is perhaps this one that presents Christians with the clearest opportunity to both proclaim and live out the gospel in public. One of the misconceptions I hear from many evangelicals about contemporary society is that most people are happy and satisfied with their autonomous moral existences and that the facet of Christian truth that must be amplified the most when preaching to this generation is the law. The problem, it is suggested, is that secular people do not believe they will be judged for their lives. The reality of judgment therefore must be pressed upon them more urgently than any other message since it is only that truth that will penetrate the sense of self-satisfaction that describes most people today.

12 Twenge, *iGen*, 251.

This is a case of offering the right solution to the wrong problem. It is absolutely true that the gospel destroys our sense of autonomy and self-righteousness by revealing God's truth, and God's wrath against those who suppress it (Rom. 1). Yet it is *not* true that the dominant characteristic of contemporary culture is one of worldly joy and satisfaction. Nearly every report of teens and young adults in the West today tells a very different story. Anxiety and depression are at all-time highs. Preteens contemplate and commit suicide. Affluent and technologically sophisticated people say they are lonelier than ever. Social media and the web pulsate with a seemingly nonstop sense of anger, frustration, and despair at the world. And young people in particular are facing something their parents never did: an online marketplace of the self, where the rewards of affirmation are perpetually counterbalanced by the threat of a pile-on.

The ambient culture is practically begging for someone to articulate a theology of repentance.

A genuinely Christian response begins by affirming, as the townspeople in *The Scarlet Letter* knew well, that guilt is real. When Adam and Eve sinned against their Creator in the garden, "the eyes of both were opened" (Gen. 3:7). Sin is no mental trick, no trauma-induced mirage. To feel the reality of sinfulness is to open your eyes and see reality for what it is. What's more, sin is the great equalizer. "For all have sinned and fall short of the glory of God" (Rom. 3:23). The awareness of sin in us destroys our spiritual and emotional confidence in ourselves, and the realization that absolutely everyone around us shares in this sinful condition likewise destroys any naivety about the world we live in. Beneath many of the outrage-fueled spectacles of social media lies a utopian dream, a desire to escape a world in which we are constantly reminded of our guilt and create a different one. The desire for such a change elicits passionate animosity toward anyone who might thwart it. "When you believe the brokenness of this world can be not just ameliorated but fixed, once and for all," writes Alan Jacobs, "then people who don't share your optimism, or who do share it but invest it in a different system, are adversaries of Utopia."[13]

In contrast, the Christian doctrine of the atonement tells us that we are powerless to absolve ourselves but that we simultaneously have an opportunity for our guilt to be truly, meaningfully, taken care of. The Christian call to repentance is not a sneakily political way to offload moral responsibility. When the online shame culture demands that people who offend must "go away," it participates in the same hypocritically utilitarian ethos that Julian Hawthorne detected in his father's novel. Christianity, on the other hand, offers a real atonement for guilt that not only takes condemnation away but results in a genuine transformation of the person from spiritually dead to spiritually alive (Eph. 2:1–10). As John Stott put it, "There is healing through the wounds of Christ, life through his death, pardon through his pain, salvation through his suffering."[14]

This experience of divine atonement and grace always results in a profound humility of spirit. It is impossible to gaze at the cross and contemplate your own significance. One reason that Christians do not fear (or should not fear) discussing ideas or opinions they disagree with is that the gospel gives them a low view of themselves but a high view of God: his power, his victory, his sovereign rule over everything. The Christian striving in the area of politics and public life is not trying to create Utopia. His opponents are not mortal enemies that must be subjugated if the good guys are to win. Rather,

13 Alan Jacobs, *How to Think: A Survival Guide for a World at Odds* (New York: Crown, 2017), 74.
14 John Stott, *Basic Christianity* (Grand Rapids, MI: Eerdmans, 1958), 99.

he is a recipient of mercy who is heralding the coming of a kingdom that is decisive. Moreover, the assurance of a final judgment by a God who is both perfectly righteous and perfectly loving is a source of lasting peace and rest. The instrument of final justice is taken out of our hands and given to the one who turned it on his Son rather than on us. This is precisely the kind of emotional, social, and spiritual balm that a shame-addled digital culture desperately needs.

Woe Is Me

Helen Andrews's story about her journey at the center of an online shame storm ends with her reflecting on its meaning. She writes that she had always believed that suffering is part of God's plan for our good, and, in fact, that "there is no belief my brush with online shaming confirmed more."

> My first reaction to the video was to feel aggrieved, thinking that I did not deserve what was happening to me, but on the Day of Judgment all my sins will be shouted from the housetops, and Todd's rant will sound like a retirement luncheon toast in comparison. Of course I deserved it, and worse; most of us poor sinners do.[15]

Part of the power of online shaming cycles is that it's not just the mob that feels their target is guilty. The target itself knows too. This is why, I think, many cultural critics scoff at the idea that a "cancel culture" even exists. Sure, they respond, some people get hounded offline; but the vast majority of people who experience this deserves it, and if the internet has redistributed the balance of

---

15   Helen Andrews, "Shame Storm."

power away from those with comfortable jobs and a lot of freedom to say or do whatever they want, all the better.

There's some truth there. Part of what cancel culture reveals is that there are many personalities and ideas and attitudes that would not survive socially if they were brought above a whisper. When text messages displaying ugly racism or sexism are broadcast, our opinion of the texter is lowered, no matter how we might object to the lack of due process. Why? Because those ideas really are sinful, they really are wicked, and they really do cause harm. There is a sense in which we can and ought to be grateful to live in a world where there is slightly less chance that evil can live and work in the halls of power unnoticed.

But just as Hester Prynne's lonely presence on the scaffold told a lie about the sin of her pastor, so too does the ritual of shaming and cancellation tell a lie about all of us. No one can watch these spectacles without feeling a quiver of fear: "What if it's me next?" What if those texts I sent, that joke I told, that relationship I misused—what if someone were to broadcast those things? Perhaps this fear even motivates us to join in the pile-on, hopeful that our virtuous display of indignation will persuade all onlookers that we can't possibly have any skeletons in our own closet. The psychological burden on modern people to both disbelieve in and yet hide their own moral guilt is crushing. It creates despair, not freedom; it poisons relationships rather than empowering them. That's why the solution must be real. It must open our eyes but not expose us utterly. It must take away what we can't wash out but without bleaching our souls. It has to burn out the impurity but not consume us.

That's why, for us, the Old Testament prophet Isaiah's vision of God's throne room is a hopeful story:

In the year that King Uzziah died I saw the Lord sitting upon a throne, high and lifted up; and the train of his robe filled the temple. Above him stood the seraphim. Each had six wings: with two he covered his face, and with two he covered his feet, and with two he flew. And one called to another and said:

> "Holy, holy, holy is the LORD of hosts;
>   the whole earth is full of his glory!"

And the foundations of the thresholds shook at the voice of him who called, and the house was filled with smoke. And I said: "Woe is me! For I am lost; for I am a man of unclean lips, and I dwell in the midst of a people of unclean lips; for my eyes have seen the King, the LORD of hosts!"

Then one of the seraphim flew to me, having in his hand a burning coal that he had taken with tongs from the altar. And he touched my mouth and said: "Behold, this has touched your lips; your guilt is taken away, and your sin atoned for" (Isa. 6:1–7).

7

Naked in the Dark

Digital Liturgy #4: Consumption

*"Do you remember that bit of rabbit, Mr. Frodo?" he
said. "And our place under the warm bank in Captain
Faramir's country, the day I saw an oliphaunt?"*

*"No, I am afraid not, Sam," said Frodo. "At least, I know
that such things happened, but I cannot see them. No
taste of food, no feel of water, no sound of wind, no
memory of tree or grass or flower, no image of moon or
star are left to me. I am naked in the dark, Sam, and
there is no veil between me and the wheel of fire. I begin
to see it even with my waking eyes, and all else fades."*

THE LORD OF THE RINGS

THROUGHOUT J. R. R. TOLKIEN'S epic fantasy novel *The Lord
of the Rings*, the militaristic, violent power of Sauron's One Ring is
alluded to but never depicted. What is depicted, forcefully through
the ruined character Gollum and more subtly through the heroic
hobbit Frodo, is the Ring's psychological power. As a living relic,

crafted by an immortal and malevolent being, the Ring exercises a vampiric influence over any who bear it for an extended time. In a manner resembling demonic possession, the Ring bearer eventually loses his sense of self as his mind itself becomes Ring-like, deadened to the things he once loved and consumed instead with the Ring. Crawling slowly up the volcanic Mount Doom, Frodo confesses to Sam that he knows he has been taken captive by the Ring's power. He cannot remember their days outside the hellish land of Mordor. He cannot choose to imagine a happier day. The Ring is possessing him, and all else feels lost.

Tolkien certainly did not intend for the One Ring to symbolize pornography. But the continuity between pornography and the Ring's powers of emotional and imaginative captivity is striking. It is impossible to talk honestly about how the internet shapes us without reflecting on the way that pornography has blazed a seemingly permanent trail through the hearts and minds of multiple generations. Not only is pornography arguably the web's chief export into the world; for many millions of people, it is a definitive feature of their relationship with the web.

While pornography certainly existed before the first personal computer ever went online, internet porn is better understood as an altogether different kind of experience than print pornography. For reasons we'll get to shortly, the nature of the web forms an astonishingly powerful complement to the function of pornography. It is not just that much pornography can be found online. It is that the web, by virtue of what it is, is intrinsically pornographically shaped.

Why Not Start Here?

Before I go further, I want to address a question that very well could be asked at this point. Why isn't this chapter 1? If the goal is to help Christians think about their relationship to the web more wisely and more biblically, and if pornography is, as I said above, arguably the web's chief export to the world, why not start with this issue and go from there? Why not start out by addressing the most urgent, most presenting problem and then later on discussing things like epistemology and outrage culture? There are reasons.

First, and perhaps most to the point for some of my readers, this is not a book about breaking free from addiction to pornography. If that's what you're looking for, God bless you for looking for help, and I have some recommendations that I sincerely believe will give you grace.[1]

Second, as we'll see in a minute, I don't believe it's possible to isolate the issue of pornography from the other digital liturgies we've seen so far. One of the core convictions of this book is that our digital tools speak to us, and evaluating *all* they say is a spiritual task. A careful consideration of Christian wisdom and the culture of the web reveals that pornography is a logical and predictable creature of the spiritual habitat of the internet. This in turn has application to how we respond personally to the temptations and habits that can so easily cling to us. If we misunderstand online pornography as an aberration that we must contain so that we can go on and live our screen-mediated lives with no guilt and no embarrassing things to tell our accountability partners, we will both miss the point of purity *and* greatly weaken our power against digital lust. Rather, we need to identify online pornography as a symptom of a greater, more systemic disease.

Finally, if discovering that this chapter is not quite a "how to quit porn" manual has tempted you to put it down and search again

1 Ray Ortlund, *The Death of Porn: Men of Integrity Building a World of Nobility* (Wheaton, IL: Crossway, 2021); Garret Kell, *Pure in Heart* (Wheaton, IL: Crossway, 2021).

for something more relevant, I'd like to remind you of something. The sea in which you're drowning is not all that's real. The power of pornography to dominate your emotions, your attention, your prayer life, and your Christian walk is not a power that deserves your support. From deep personal experience, I can testify that one of the most powerful steps that anyone can take out from porn addiction is to realize that there is far more to your Christian identity and your walk with Christ than how many days it's been since your last slip-up. You and I are free to think, pray, and read about other things. In fact, given the command we have from our Savior to obey "all" that he has commanded, we must do this. You may be swimming for your life in the depths. Take heart: this is not merely a world of water. There is land, even if you can't see it right now.

The Web's Chief Export

Few people demand evidence that there's a lot of pornography online. Yet the statistics themselves are still sobering. According to web research hub Statista, three of the top twenty most visited websites in the world are "adult" sites, accounting for over four billion visits in a single month.[2] It should be remembered that the Apple App Store, as of this writing, still forbids any openly pornographic content. This means that whereas sites like Google, Facebook, and Twitter can be accessed via apps, the billions of hits that porn sites receive each month come from people who have to manually navigate to the site on their computer or mobile device.

The sheer ubiquity of pornography online and the general failure of existing measures to prevent children from accessing it have led to a cultural interrogation in some parts of the world. During his

---

2   "Most Popular Websites Worldwide as of November 2021, by Total Visits," Statista, accessed November 14, 2022, https://www.statista.com/.

term as British Prime Minister, David Cameron commissioned his government to enact policies requiring internet companies to block access to pornography. Cameron observed, "Children can't go into the shops or the cinema and buy things meant for adults or have adult experiences; we rightly regulate to protect them. But when it comes to the internet, in the balance between freedom and responsibility we've neglected our responsibility to children."[3] Similar governmental measures have happened in the United States, with some states declaring pornography a public health crisis. Even many secular media outlets are beginning to wonder aloud if modern culture is too pornified. A 2016 *Time* magazine cover story featured testimonies of several young men whose porn addictions have damaged their lives, and celebrities like Billie Eilish have spoken transparently and forcefully about how early exposure to pornography warped their view of relationships and sex.

While it may be tempting to think of these developments as part of a culture-wide conservative resurgence on sexuality, there's little evidence to believe that. A better interpretation is that the power and availability of online pornography have far exceeded most people's expectations. Online porn has not stayed in either its "adults only" or "consent" cages. It is easily accessed by children and teens, and it frequently depicts people (especially young women) in various stages of humiliation and abuse. Perhaps most importantly, smartphone and tablet technologies have made accessing pornography easier, faster, and more secretive, which in turn tends to strengthen addiction and make quitting far more difficult.

---

3   David Cameron, "The Internet and Pornography: Prime Minister Calls for Action," speech, 2010 to 2015 Conservative and Liberal Democrat Coalition Government, updated July 24, 2013, https://www.gov.uk/.

Thus, the vast majority of secular discussions or efforts regarding pornography focus almost exclusively on trying to put it back into its "adults only" and "consent only" box. Not only is this an obviously non-Christian approach; it is doomed to failure for a more elemental reason. A large part of online pornography's power over contemporary culture comes from the devices that deliver it. There's an important synergy between the logic and structure of the web itself and that of pornography. This is obviously not to say that everything on the internet is pornographic, or that people who are on the web a lot are always going to end up viewing porn. But it is to say that the habits, feelings, and ideas that the web makes more plausible—to use Neil Postman's phrase, the way the web "re-stages the world"[4]—are the same habits, feelings, and ideas at work in the person who is hooked on porn. Put differently, the internet is pornographically shaped.

To see this clearly, we can focus on three characteristics of the web that find particularly sharp expression in online porn: novelty, consumption, and isolation.

Novelty

Perhaps one of the most profound summaries of life in an online age is comedian Bo Burnham's song "Welcome to the Internet." Burnham captures, in both lyric and melody, the chaotic nature of the web's enormity. Whatever you want, you can find it online. As Burnham's song artfully (even disturbingly) captures, there's no desire, no psychosis, no far-flung curiosity, or even no antihuman instinct so strange that there's not some kind of content for it. And what makes Burnham's song especially insightful is the realization

---

4   Neil Postman, *Amusing Ourselves to Death* (New York: Penguin, 1985).

that the web is not simply a passive menu that delivers what we ask for. The chaos itself seems to sink its claws into us, making us curious for things we don't even really care about, vulnerable to distractions and temptations we'd never come near away from the screen.

Nearly every user of social media has experienced what we might call the "bored scroll" or the "mindless refresh." This is what happens when we keep scrolling or keep refreshing our feeds for no other reason than finding new content that such purposeless attention might reveal. This type of behavior is not an accident, by the way; it is a product of specific design choices of the web, an example of how technology is always shaping us. "Infinite scroll," for example, is a neurologically influenced web tool that rewards users as they dive deeper into the feed, guaranteeing new sights and sounds as the page reemerges.[5] Such tools are only possible precisely because the web is an endless novelty machine. Whether it's the ever-expanding borders of YouTube and Wikipedia or the never-ending returns on the most obscure Google searches, the web is inherently designed to deliver, in the words of Burnham's song, "everything, all of the time."

The web's nature as a novelty machine, however, is intrinsic to its nature as a pornographic medium. There is a vital connection between aimless immersion in "content" and the spiritual mood that primes a heart to seek out lust. Whereas in film and romance novels, lust is almost always a sin of passion and decisiveness, many who immerse in online pornography do so not because their desires are too strong but because they are too weak. Emotionally numbed by endless scrolling, the human heart tends to become inclined

5   See Hal Koss, "Infinite Scroll: What Is It Good For?," BuiltIn, January 7, 2021, https://built in.com/.

toward that which simply offers a dash of color to an otherwise drab listlessness. In other words, the mindless search for more *stuff* pushes us toward the temporary thrill and pseudo-connection of online porn. One Christian writer connects pornography addiction to the ancient sin of acedia, a spiritual torpor or boredom that comes from a loss of meaning. "What is to be learned from the testimonies of pornography's users is the important fact that, contrary to prevailing cultural assumptions, the lust of the eyes is not a 'hot' but rather a 'cold' vice," he writes. "It arises from the roaming unrest of the spirit rooted in a spiritual apathy."[6] Like King David wandering the roof of his palace during the season when kings should have been off to war, our modern encounters with online pornography can be a reflection of a much larger immersion in purposelessness—a problem that usually begins not with explicit images but with meaningless scrolls.

Consumption

The near-infinite novelties of the internet do not exist simply to hide. They are made, of course, to be consumed. Consumption is arguably the core ethos of the online age. It is revealed in the contemporary lingo that's used to describe human activity online. We "binge" TV shows on our streaming services. We "stalk" others on social media. The singular word *content* is now used to describe any- and everything that is published on the internet, a word that suggests not something definite that demands a particular response (an essay to be read, a photograph to be admired, etc.), but a morass of generic attention-soaking material. Anything can be content because anything can be consumed.

---

6   Reinhard Hutter, "Pornography and Acedia," *First Things*, April 2012, https://www.first things.com/.

One of the more vivid examples of this is YouTube. While many of us go to YouTube for quick access to big cultural artifacts, like music videos or movie trailers, the heartbeat of YouTube's business is its "content creators." What is most astonishing about the content of YouTube is how seemingly all-encompassing it is. If you can imagine someone doing something (something that won't get them arrested, at least), you can almost certainly find a YouTube video of that very thing. Gone are the days where the most watched videos were always the best amateur singers or athletes. Now, one of the biggest genres of YouTube "content" is the reaction video, which usually features ordinary, everyday people doing exactly what the term suggests: reacting. They're reacting to anything and everything from movies, to surgeries, to police dashcam footage, and just about anything else you can dream up. Fifteen years ago, it would have been almost impossible to convince people that they could make real money by recording their facial reactions and letting other people watch them. Today, though, even basic human interaction is a valuable commodity, consumable at will.

The web's ethos of consumption is a fitting vehicle for the pornography industry. Pornography is, after all, fundamentally a consumptive act, a transformation of human persons into soulless objects of spectacle. Porn and the web go together so efficiently precisely because they are both instruments of commodification, a way to turn the most intimate or even most elementary stuff of human life into consumable content. Consider how the term *porn* has even been repurposed to refer to images that make something desirable. There are now entire sections of the web dedicated to "food porn," meaning photos of delicious dishes. In the world of "food porn," it's the image that's meant to be consumed, not the food depicted. There are also communities dedicated to "earth porn," meaning pictures and videos of beautiful scenery. Pornography's function as a way to turn the transcendent into the consumable has become so embedded into our online lives that it is now literally what we can call any of the content we consume. It's almost as if, in at least a real sense, everything on the internet is a kind of porn.

Isolation

It turns out that the most efficient way to consume the web's novelties is not as a member of a thick community of meaningful relationships but as an isolated individual. Internet technology's trajectory over the past decade has been inarguably bent toward the solitary individual, reachable at any point for any reason.

Consider three major phases of how civilization has logged online. We could consider these as three distinct chapters in the life of the web: the lab, the living room, and the pocket. What we know as the modern internet began in the mid-twentieth century as a sophisticated and highly technical attempt to link computer systems for scientific, government, and military purposes. Like the massive, room-filling supercomputers used by NASA that were depicted in the film *Hidden Figures*, the early states of internet technology were overwhelming in their scope and prowess. It took exceptionally well-educated people long hours and much effort to even maintain the simplest of networks.

But the emergence of the personal computer and the modem transformed the internet's relationship to the world and gave birth eventually to what we now know as the web. As personal computers became cheaper, faster, and more important to work and recreation, the web eventually became a part of people's homes. A computer and a phone line were all that were required to connect a living room to a seemingly infinite world. But, importantly, even in this phase, the computer and the phone line were required. Experiencing the internet was an experience that entailed being at a particular place and doing particular things. To this day, "computer labs" at universities testify to how the web was experienced for several years.

Eventually, however, the web entered its third, current, and most revolutionary state: the smartphone. With the smartphone, the importance of place in experiencing the web is nearly obliterated. No longer must you seek out a dedicated space, with a particular set of wires plugged into a particular set of ports. Now, thanks to mobile technology, *you* are the place. Whether in the car or in the airplane, at school or at church, the web is with you, accessible as quickly as you can reach into your pocket.

The net effect has been that the web is now primarily experienced in isolation. We don't huddle around the family PC to see the new photos from NASA's telescope; by the time we assemble for dinner, we've all seen the pictures on our own curated newsfeeds. Streaming apps offer multiple profiles so that each person can stream individually. With this great individualism, however, has come a palpable sense of aloneness. Though we are more entertained and curated than ever before, many modern people report stunning levels of loneliness and inability to meaningfully relate to others. Connectivity has undermined connection.

The Web Is Pornographically Shaped

In his excellent book *You Are Not Your Own: Belonging to God in an Inhuman World*, Alan Noble makes the important observation that online pornography is not just an act of lust. It's an act of power. Computers have given the human craving for novelty and consumption an unprecedented ability to manufacture anything, involving anyone, at any time. This is why Noble says that "the internet has changed pornography":

> Consider the power of choice. Today you can find a pornographic depiction of virtually any fantasy. If you can dream it, you can find it. And you can probably find it for free within three minutes. When you inevitably get bored of that fantasy, just dispose of it and find something new—indefinitely. Humans have always been able to imagine all kinds of sexual scenarios, but we haven't been able to make them exist, unless you happened to be a tremendously powerful despotic ruler. We all have the power of Caligula now.[7]

"Contemporary pornography puts the individual user at the center of the universe," Noble concludes. "We have a godlike freedom to pursue any fantasy we wish."[8] He's right. But we should notice something important. The power to find anything you want to see, the access to a never-ending supply of new consumables, and the limitless freedom to make fantasy become reality—these are not just characteristics of online *porn* but of the online world in general. Suppose it is not pornography we are talking about. Suppose instead the subject were self-help advice or life gurus. Would anything in Noble's paragraph above cease to be true if the references to pornography were swapped out? Of course not. We could even replace pornography with, say, Christian teaching. Yet it would still be true that the modern

---

7   Alan Noble, *You Are Not Your Own: Belonging to God in an Inhuman Age* (Downers Grove, IL: InterVarsity Press, 2021), 64.
8   Noble, *You Are Not Your Own*, 65.

web user has a godlike freedom to pursue any kind of Christian teaching they want. It would still be true that the "normal" rhythms and habits of online life would be to find something to suit you, use it until it becomes boring, and then move onto something else. In other words, the worldview that undergirds use of online pornography is the same worldview that lies underneath the entire web.

Again, I should make clear what I am not saying. I'm not saying that *everything* on the web is pornographic, nor am I saying that everyone who spends a significant amount of time online is secretly looking at pornography or will soon. To say that the web is pornographically shaped is not to say that it is inherently explicit or sinful. Rather, the point is that the digital liturgies of endless novelty, constant consumption, and limitless power make pornography more plausible to our hearts and our habits. Within the web's spiritual habitat, looking at pornography makes sense and feels natural. This not only has implications for how we think about our relationship to digital technology as a whole; it means very important things for how we disciple each other in the fight against lust, a fight that for many Christians feels incredibly hopeless and permanent.

It also helps to explain why, culturally, our efforts to keep pornography within a "consenting adults only" box have failed so miserably. You won't find any sane CEO of a tech company that says it's a good thing for children to be exposed early to hardcore pornography. You won't find any politicians who argue that eight-year-olds should be allowed to learn about sex and their bodies from those websites. Everyone agrees that children should not encounter this stuff. Yet encounter it they do, by greater and greater numbers each year. Why? The pornographic shape of the web is the best and simplest explanation. Online pornography won't stay in its box because the box is designed for it to escape.

One of the most disturbing examples of this I've seen in recent years was in a multipart investigation by the *Wall Street Journal* into the social media app TikTok. The *Journal's* reporters discovered that TikTok's algorithm, a highly sophisticated system for the app to learn more about users to tailor more content to them, was programmed to capture even momentary pauses of scrolling. If a user is scrolling through a selection of videos, even *slowing* the scroll on one particular video triggers the algorithm to recommend more videos like that. The *Journal* set up dummy accounts on the app and programmed the accounts to accept certain recommendations. Several of the accounts ended up spending hours on obscure and fringe channels, many of which were sexually explicit. The *Journal* found that the TikTok algorithm pushed several accounts toward the more suggestive and "adult" content, even though none of this content was initially recommended. The accounts were led gradually, recommendation by recommendation, to a corner of TikTok that was clearly more extreme than the norm.[9]

Even in the places of the web that are moderated and purportedly kept safe for younger audiences, online pornography tends to get the upper hand. Part of this, of course, is a failure of parents to know what's going on with their kids' phones. Part of it is surely a moral abrogation of duty on the part of tech companies to resist profiting by objectification. But it is also the web itself at work: a spiritual habitat that makes life itself consumable and malleable in any way you desire.

9   "Inside TikTok's Algorithm: A WSJ Video Investigation," *Wall Street Journal*, July 21, 2012, https://www.wsj.com/.

In the Sunlight

A make-believe world of endless novelty, limitless consumption, and godlike power can cast a powerful spell. But in the end, its joys mold. The era of online pornography has not resulted in a more liberated, more sexually adventurous generation, but in something very close to the opposite. Contemporary sociologists are observing what they call the "Great Sex Recession," a demographic-shifting trend whereby emerging adults, especially Gen-Z, are failing to pair up, failing to marry, even failing to have sex. Meanwhile, against the backdrop of the #MeToo movement, many young American adults are expressing confusion and even fear about relationships and sex. Near the center of this stagnation of American adulthood lies online pornography, captivating millions of young men who cannot escape its lures, and an increasing number of young women for whom the fabrications and misrepresentations of pornography have become normal yet crushing expectations on their own bodies.

And yet behind online pornography lies a structure seemingly designed to prop it up. Pornographic content is searing consciences and exploiting victims around the world, but the spirit behind the content is the same spirit of commodification and consumption that rules unopposed often in our own lives. Just as online porn invites users into a seemingly risk-free fantasy to consume beautiful bodies without any rejection or commitment, the web itself helps to grow this fantasy in our hearts as we consume identities, ideas, opinions, and even one another in lonely isolation.

These digital liturgies are powerful precisely because they tend to absorb more and more of our attention in our computerized lives. But the spiritual habitats they create hold a much looser grip on our hearts when we spend time outside them. In the last several years

I have talked to a large number of men who struggle with online pornography. I've also spoken to a striking number of men who, while certainly not above the temptation, have never experienced a meaningful season of defeat in this area. While many things about these two groups vary, one consistent pattern has been that the men who struggle with online porn tend to spend a lot of time online generally, while the men who don't struggle in that way tend to spend more time offline. I don't believe this is because avoiding social media makes you more holy. I believe it's because a regular immersion in the world of the web does work on our hearts, makes us thirsty for something that will excite and ennoble us, and shrinks the size of our world so that these imaginary lovers somehow seem more real.

It's when we exit this spiritual habitat that we can see these illusions for what they are.

Proximity tends to determine plausibility. In Proverbs 7, Solomon observes a "young man lacking sense" (v. 7) who ends up committing adultery. What causes his downfall? His problems start not with sex but with location. He is pictured "passing along the street near [a woman's] corner, taking the road to her house in the twilight, in the evening, at the time of night and darkness" (7:8–9). The entire reason he hears the adulteress's "seductive speech" (v. 21) is that he decides to go near her home at a time of day when his desire is strong and the day is dying. Would it have been possible for him to resist even then? Certainly. But it would have been much easier for him to resist in the broad daylight, in the company of neighbors, where the stupidity of adultery feels obvious. The simple man's decision to pass by her home at twilight was a decision to enter a particular habitat that made lust look like something it's not.

God's good, given world subverts the charms of lust. The moments of weakness are the moments of listless anxiety in which we hope that something we find online can distract us or flatter us just enough. They are not the moments when we are surrounded by the beauty of snow-capped mountains or snow-white beaches or the friends and family we love most. In those moments we are brought out of ourselves; most of the time, the thought of aimlessly scrolling at such a moment feels absurd, even immoral. Similarly, we don't bring a raging desire for godlike freedom to our computers when we feel that kind of deeply satisfied weariness from a day well spent, making and studying and serving in a way we know contributed something from God to those around us. Instead, that desire bubbles up in us after days and perhaps weeks of being trapped in our own minds, frustrated by the smallness of everyday life, or fearful that no one really sees or knows us. Living, working, studying, and loving in the sun of God's embodied creation, feeling a sense of transcendent purpose and meaning to even our "ordinary" days, is what makes the mirage of online pornography feel small, even silly.

Perhaps this is why the New Testament so often contrasts sexual immorality not with stoic resistance but with love. In the famous "put off, put on" passage of Colossians 3, Paul says that Christians must "put to death therefore what is earthly in you: sexual immorality, impurity, passion, evil desire, and covetousness, which is idolatry" (v. 5). In the parallel follow-up passage on what Christians must "put on," Paul writes:

Put on then, as God's chosen ones, holy and beloved, compassionate hearts, kindness, humility, meekness, and patience, bearing with one another and, if one has a complaint against another, forgiving each other; as the Lord has forgiven you, so you also must forgive. And above all these put on love, which binds everything together in perfect harmony. And let the peace of Christ rule in your hearts, to which indeed you were called in one body. And be thankful. Let the word of Christ dwell in you richly, teaching and admonishing one another in all wisdom, singing psalms and hymns and spiritual songs, with thankfulness in your hearts to God. (vv. 12–16)

The alternative to sexual immorality and impurity is compassion, kindness, humility, meekness, and patience. It's forgiveness and love and gratitude, teaching and singing. You know what all those things involve? Other people. Here is where the plague of pornography and the digital liturgy of consumption overlap. They are both heart cavities that God's word would have us fill with love. It takes a humble confession that we need to know and be known by others, that we need faces and voices to encourage, rebuke, and grieve with us. To be sure, socialization alone doesn't magically cure lust or help us keep technology in its proper place. But the darkness of addiction, both sexual and electronic, will not abide the sunlight coming through the open window.

One of my favorite quotes on this topic comes from pastor John Piper. In a sermon he preached in 1990, Piper got to the heart of how the light of God's good world can heal us from the illusions of pornography. Though he said these words before most people had even seen the internet, they are perhaps even more relevant now than then:

Do you know why there are no windows on adult book stores? Or do you know why there are no windows on certain kinds of nightclubs in the city? I suppose your answer would be, "Well, because they don't want people looking in and getting a free sight." That is not the only reason. You know why? Because they don't want people looking out at the sky. You know why? The sky is the enemy of lust. I just ask you to think back on your struggles. The sky is a great power against lust. Pure, lovely, wholesome, powerful, large-hearted things cannot abide the soul of a sexual fantasy at the same time.

I remember as I struggled with these things in my teenage years and in my college years. I knew how I could fight most effectively in those days. Now I have developed other strategies over the years that have proved very effective. And one way of fighting was simply to get out of the dark places—get out of the lonely rooms. Get out of the boxed-in places. Get out of the places where it is just small—me and my mind and my imagination, what I can do with it—and get to where I am just surrounded by color and beauty and bigness and loveliness. . . . There is something about bigness, something about beauty that helps battle against the puny, small, cruddy use of the mind to fantasize about sexual things.[10]

There is indeed something about bigness. It's what we were made for. It's *whom* we were made for.

---

10 John Piper, "Do You See the Joy of God in the Sun? Part 2," Desiring God, August 26, 1990, https://www.desiringgod.org/.

Death by Minutiae

Digital Liturgy #5: Meaninglessness

*There is darkness without, and when I die there will
be darkness within. There is no splendour, no vastness
anywhere, only triviality for a moment, and then nothing.*

BERTRAND RUSSELL

HAD THE ATHEIST PHILOSOPHER Bertrand Russell lived to see
the age of the internet, his judgment that all of existence boils
down to "triviality for a moment" would not likely have changed.[1]
Convinced there is no God, no afterlife, and nothing eternally
real, Russell sensed toward the end of his life that consciousness
itself was little more than a joke. Given the presuppositions, who
can disagree? If matter is all that exists, the biological cessation of
functions in one's body is the end of everything. Work, leisure,

---

1   Bertrand Russell, *Autobiography* (New York: Routledge, 1998), 393.

relationships, thinking, learning, and even love will evaporate with the firing of the last neuron. How can one look into the abyss that is 99.9 percent of human history and not chalk every gift, every pleasure, every moment of hope to meaningless triviality?

Most of the people living in the world today do not share Russell's atheism, and even most of those who do would stop short of describing all of life as "triviality for a moment." Gloomy philosophical nihilism is a tough sell. But the feeling that Russell describes in this line is not, in fact, very hard to understand at all. In fact, there is much reason to believe that the feeling that life is dark and meaningless is one of the fastest-growing sentiments in the developed West today. Its ascendance is testified to by the astonishing rise of diagnosed anxiety and depression, particularly among the young. According to the Suicide Prevention Research Center, the rate of teenage suicide has increased to nearly fifteen per one hundred thousand among those aged fifteen to twenty-four years old. In 2020 suicide was the second most common cause of death among those aged ten to fourteen and the third most common cause of death for those fifteen to twenty-four.[2]

Almost everyone who researches this data wants to know why. Why have the young—those with all their lives ahead of them, those with everything to look forward to—started to despair of life? It's not easy to find agreement on this question. Some cultural analysts go immediately to economics, suggesting that millennials and Gen-Z are the first generation in American history to have bleaker economic prospects than their parents. Others point to national traumas, such as September 11, the 2008 financial crisis, or the COVID-19 pandemic, that may have instilled a certain

2   "Suicide by Age," Suicide Prevention Research Center, accessed November 14, 2022, https://www.sprc.org/.

hopelessness or fear into emerging adults. And many Christians have responded to the surge of self-harm among young adults by lamenting the loss of religion in the public square, which has robbed the young of a sense of transcendent identity and purpose in life.

It's important to observe that all three of these explanations are plausible and even complementary. People who do not believe that their work or education will make a meaningful difference in the quality of their lives will understandably start to question the meaning of that work or education. World-reorienting events do have a way of unsettling us and making us less hopeful about the future. Over against the unpredictable and traumatizing nature of reality, the hope of an eternal God and life after death provides a comfort and confidence that secularism simply cannot replace. All of these factors are undoubtedly at work in Western culture today.

Yet there is another, less-discussed possibility. As researchers such as Jean Twenge have shown, there is a sharp and impossible-to-miss correlation between the rise of self-reported mental health crises among teens and young adults, and the availability and use of smartphone technology. Paradoxically, the growth and popularity of social media platforms have been accompanied by massive increases of those who say they are lonely and cut off from others. In a modern society that is literally defined by its connectivity, an enormous number of people feel themselves cut off: from meaningful work and relationships and from a stabilizing purpose to their lives. The ambient web's invasion of all areas of our daily lives, which on the surface promises to be a vehicle of friendship, efficiency, and entertainment, has turned out instead to be a vehicle for a very specific kind of despair: a kind that we could label, with apologies to Bertrand Russell, "triviality for a moment, and then nothing."

"I Used to Be a Human Being"

Perhaps no piece of writing has illustrated the power of the digital age to induce this kind of despair better than Andrew Sullivan's 2016 essay, "I Used to Be a Human Being." As one of the earliest and most prolific political bloggers on the entire internet, Sullivan built a serious and lucrative career as an online writer. For decades, Sullivan scoured the web daily for the most interesting, most relevant, most reaction-provoking material he could find, frequently responding to it on his blog with posts that ranged from a sentence or two to several thousand words. Sullivan writes that he was "a very early adopter of what we might call now living-in-the-web," a pattern that intensified through the years as sites like Facebook and Twitter seemed to "house" content, and refreshing and rescouring those platforms for the latest thing to know about became an integral part of the day.

Weeks, months, and years of day-in, day-out internet presence launched Sullivan to greater success as a blogger than virtually anyone else. But eventually he realized that something was wrong. His mind was beginning to become internet-shaped, a transformation evident in the way that analog life felt almost impossible:

> I tried reading books, but that skill now began to elude me. After a couple of pages, my fingers twitched for a keyboard. I tried meditation, but my mind bucked and bridled as I tried to still it. I got a steady workout routine, and it gave me the only relief I could measure for an hour or so a day. But over time in this pervasive virtual world, the online clamor grew louder and louder. Although I spent hours each day, alone and silent, attached to a laptop, it felt as if I were in a constant cacophonous crowd of

words and images, sounds and ideas, emotions and tirades—
a wind tunnel of deafening, deadening noise. So much of it was
irresistible, as I fully understood. So much of the technology
was irreversible, as I also knew. But I'd begun to fear that this
new way of living was actually becoming a way of not-living.[3]

As Sullivan recounts in the essay, his nonstop immersion in
digital environments had the unintended but very serious effect of
making quiet, solitude, and stillness painful. Sullivan's story ends
with his seeking refuge at a modern monastery, in counseling ses-
sions for the "extreme pain" that accompanied his separation from
his devices. Fascinatingly, the essay ends on a note not of personal
transformation but of frustration. Sullivan acknowledges that his
newfound habits of meditation are almost impossible to practice
consistently now that he's surrounded again by digital connectivity.
Speaking to himself as much as anyone else, Sullivan concludes,
"The threat is to our souls. At this rate, if the noise does not relent,
we might even forget we have any."[4]

Sullivan is an unusually vivid and articulate writer. But the experience he's describing is not unusual. In fact, among friends my age,
these slow-burning feelings of being trapped in an invisible noise
chamber are the norm. More and more, we commiserate with one
another about how difficult it is to finish books, how distracted and
tied to our phones we feel around our children, and how restless our
minds and emotions are unless we can scroll. These feelings are so
commonly shared now that there are entire products and services
devoted simply to helping people not use their devices (I've used

3 Andrew Sullivan, "I Used to Be a Human Being," *New York Magazine*, September 19, 2016,
   https://nymag.com/.
4 Sullivan, "I Used to Be a Human Being."

one such antidistraction app during the writing of this book!). At every turn, even as our use of the web, social media, streaming, and other digital distractions increases, so too does our awareness that the "noise" is doing something to our souls.

Despite how normal digital immersion has become in contemporary life, we seem unable to shake the feeling that something profoundly abnormal is happening to us. The title of Sullivan's essay is profound; many of us seem to remember a time, at some point in our lives, when we just didn't hear the noise the way we do now. We remember days and weeks and months without comparing our lives to strangers or wrestling with the insecurity of not measuring up. We remember a time when we could enjoy good things without having to photograph or broadcast them. We remember, somehow, what it felt like to lose ourselves in something outside us, to have our attention drawn to something that was really happening: the joy that comes from a genuine self-forgetfulness. And while those experiences still happen, they seem harder than ever to find, and all the while the anxiety and guilt and frustration of feeling like we're somehow less human than we used to be drives us back to the screen, back to the feed where we can at least stop thinking for a minute.

The *American Heritage Dictionary* defines *minutiae* as "small or trivial details."[5] As you can probably tell, this is where we get the word *minute*. You can pronounce *minute* two different ways: "my-noot" indicates something so small you can barely tell it's real ("If you stare closely you can see these minute scratches on the furniture"), while "min-it" is, of course, sixty seconds. So in its etymological fullness, minutiae evokes the idea not just of spatial

---

5   *American Heritage Dictionary*, 4th ed. (New York: Random House, 2001), s.v. "minutiae."

smallness but of a very small amount of time. Minutiae is fleetingness. It is the "mist" of our lives, according to the apostle James (James 4:14). Put together, minutiae—the minute details of our days, and the minutes that measure them—makes up the stuff of life. But in isolation, minutiae is fleeting: here one minute (literally) and gone the next.

It's easy to vilify minutiae, especially in our youth. Several years ago I read a fable about a young man who was bored with the tedious details of his life. He spent each day dreaming about what he would do tomorrow. He wanted to experience life's "highs" and felt that the burdensome minutes of school and chores were getting in the way. One day a mysterious stranger offered him a magical ball of yarn. If he only pulled on the yarn, the young man could make time move faster. During a particularly boring stretch of school, the young man pulled on the yarn and was instantly transported to the end of the school day. This experience proved addictive, and soon the young man was pulling more and more thread so he could "skip ahead" to the best parts of his life. He eventually ran out of yarn, and, as an old man who had few memories because of all he had skipped, he lamented his decision to miss out on the ordinary joys of life.

This fable has resonated with me for years. But as I get older, especially in a digital age, I find that my temptation is close to the opposite now. Instead of wanting to skip ahead, I tend to live in a social media habitat where every little update, every little argument, every little new announcement captivates my attention and hardly lets go. I find that it's not the most meaningful moments of life that elicit my strongest thoughts and emotions, but the latest online "thing," whether it involves me ("How could that person say that?") or not ("How can that person do/believe/be friends with someone who does or believes that?"). Notifications excite me even when a friend's invitation doesn't. The same clip on YouTube somehow appeals to me again and again even when that new unread book sits inches away. Like Andrew Sullivan, I often feel besieged by *noise*. We live in an age of minutiae, displayed on minute devices that take our minds and hearts captive, not years at a time, but minute by fleeting minute.

The Minutiae of Distraction, Discontentment, and Dislocation

The ambient web is a thick source of minutiae. By this, I do not mean that significant, even life-changing, things cannot take place online. Certainly they can. But it's important to understand that our normal, daily rhythms and habits are far more shaped by the trivialities of the web than by these kinds of moments. The transformation of the cell phone over the past few decades illustrates this. Around the year 2000, the vast majority of mobile phones looked like what they were: devices for interpersonal communication. Flip phones are built to make natural contact with the user's ear and mouth. By contrast, the large glass faces of smartphones are designed to be *looked* at. A smartphone's screen presents the user with dozens of apps, the majority of which do not put the user into closer communication with someone else than a phone call would, and many of which do not put the user into contact with others at all. This is another illustration of how *design* shapes *meaning*. A big reason our phones are factories of distracting minutiae is that they are built to be that.

It's not uncommon to hear modern people talk about how distracted they feel. Like so many others, I've had to confront the problem of distraction in parenting. It seems nearly every day that at some point I will find myself mindlessly thumbing through my phone while my children beg for attention. It's shameful to admit how easy it is to ignore cries of "Play with me" or "Daddy, look at this," even when there's nothing remotely worthy of my focus going on. In fact, if I'm being honest, that's the case most of the time. A great deal of the attention I grant to the web is unsolicited: there's nothing that merits my turning to it; it's just *what I do*. Nothing about this particular email demands an immediate response; in fact, it may not demand any response at all. Nothing about this particular Instagram or Twitter post needs to be seen right now. In all likelihood it will be there tomorrow, and the next day, probably even next year.

I'm currently writing this chapter in a coffee shop in my home city of Louisville, Kentucky. In the course of this particular writing session, several times (at least half a dozen) I have stopped writing and opened up a sports website, Twitter, or Amazon. Nothing new is happening with my favorite teams right now. I'm actually on a self-imposed lockout of Twitter and do not have my password, and the package I'm expecting from Amazon has said the same thing for the last several hours: "Expected today." I wish I could say that these momentary wanderings are simply necessary breaks for my eyes. But there's a huge window less than four feet in front of me, looking out into one of the busiest intersections in town. It's not that my wandering attention span has nowhere else to go. It's that digital environments beckon to me in a particularly powerful way.

The restlessness we feel when we instinctively reach for our devices ports all too easily into how we think about our lives. The distraction we fall into quickly morphs into discontent: an anxious sense of impatience with the mundane, quiet, unremarkable parts of life. The next scroll of Instagram brings picture after picture of beautiful families, happy vacations, and stunning experiences. As our attention zooms in, we feel that these photos symbolize something that's wrong with us. That family is not ours; that vacation is unaffordable; that experience is impossible. It's important to note how encountering these kinds of images on social media is different from encountering them in, say, a magazine or TV show. We may indeed feel that we don't measure up to the glamour we see in those places, but both the magazine and TV show are supposed to be snapshots of a different kind of life. We know when we pick up the issue or turn on the channel that what we're seeing is not normal life.

Social media is different. Social media is designed to feel like real life. This is why "lifestyle influencers" are paid enormous sums to advertise products—because their followers don't see them as implausible celebrity culture but as part of *normal* life. Because the web has become integrated so closely with our day-to-day work, friendships, education, and entertainment, and because the web is ambient (meaning that it's in our pockets all the time rather than on a TV or movie screen that we have to seek out in order to experience), the world that social media brings to us feels like part of our world, even if we technically know that much of the content we see on there is advertisements that have been carefully planned and produced to elicit this reaction. To go back to the language of habitats: the web is a habitat of discontentment that makes our feelings of insecurity and unhappiness seem more plausible than they might otherwise appear.

More subtle and perhaps even more important than discontentment, however, is the web's minutiae of *dislocation*. Distraction and discontentment are serious challenges to a life of Christian wisdom. But both are really symptoms, not causes. Behind the life of distraction and discontentment is the life of dislocation, by which I mean a life in which deep belonging and rootedness feel like a disadvantage, and scattered, shallow omnipresence feels like power. Dislocation happens when we are not really where we are. That sentence is not a typo. When we are physically present somewhere from which we are emotionally, mentally, and relationally absent, dislocation occurs. Dislocation is the logic of imprisonment; we believe that a just punishment for committing a major crime is not to be starved or beaten but simply dislocated, to be forced to be physically present against our will. Dislocation is why we get homesick. We sense that we are not where we belong.

Human beings are not designed to feel dislocated. Our innate need to be where we really are, to find home, is a major theme of Scripture. After Adam and Eve fell, they were exiled out of the place of their creation, the place where they were commissioned to work on behalf of God. God's people experience wandering and exile, sometimes for punishment, sometimes for testing, but always with the attendant reminder that there really is a place for them, even if they haven't reached it yet.

This struggle against dislocation and thirst for the place we really belong isn't just an effect of sin.[6] It's part of what it means to be human. This is how we are made. Earlier we saw that embodiment is part of God's grand design for his image-bearing people, and thus our bodies are crucial in our quest to flourish under divine wisdom. Because we are embodied people, we are, as a result, *locationed* people—people created to inhabit certain places in certain ways that our bodies reveal to us. John Kleinig makes the point beautifully:

---

6 Portions of this section are adapted from my Substack article "Our Bodies Tell Us What We Are," March 23, 2022, https://samueldjames.substack.com/.

Our bodies were designed to work with others and with God here on earth. They were made to be receptive and active: receptive in obtaining life from God and active in working with God to promote life here on earth. Each body has received different characteristics and abilities because each body has something different to do. Thus, my male body qualifies me to work as a husband to my wife, a father to my children, and a grandfather to my grandchildren. Unlike me, the body of a single woman qualifies her to serve as a female relative, a female friend, and a female caregiver to others. . . . We all have different vocations according to our location in the world and in our society. My location as a man is in my marriage and my family in the city of Adelaide, Australia. That is where God has appointed me to work with him caring for my wife, children, and grandchildren. He employs me to work with him in that location with those people.[7]

This is a particular way of understanding one's identity. Instead of delving deep into self-analysis and introspection to determine what we want our identity to be, we can *receive* an identity based on physical realities that are objectively true of us. These realities tie us to ourselves, our work, our place, and our relationships. Right now, because of who and where my body is, I can serve as a husband to a wife and a father to two children in Louisville, Kentucky. I cannot serve as a single man or a wife. I cannot live like a childless man or a man of grown children. And I cannot live elsewhere than where I am. I am here, I am a husband and a father, and my body tells me this.

7   John Kleinig, *Wonderfully Made: A Protestant Theology of the Body* (Bellingham, WA: Lexham Press, 2021), 50–51.

But what if modern technology can arrange things so that I can constantly move from place to place physically, not tied to any particular neighborhood, always potentially mobile? What if modern technology could separate my attention from my body geographically so that while I sit in one place, I am actually thinking and speaking and learning and working in another? This could make us feel as if the concept of place were obsolete.

We don't have to wonder. This scenario is what's happening right now. The internet has become everyone's personal airplane window seat, offering an obstructed but captivating glance at the outside world that makes our current whereabouts feel as ephemeral and temporary as a nonstop flight. That's why we feel inexplicably invested in arguments between people we don't know, about topics we don't care about. That's why we can hardly experience a crisp fall evening or a sorely needed dinner date without reaching for our phones, hoping to see some notification that brings us news from afar. Our addiction to distraction and our struggle against discontentment are both really expressions of the fact that our devices have made us feel elsewhere than we really are. We are split in two, dividing our attention and our lives. And in our quietest, most honest moments, we know the day-in, day-out burden of living this way is not sustainable. It's not what we're meant for.

Here's the good news: this feeling is itself evidence that we don't have to live this way. C. S. Lewis believed that our most fundamental desires reveal, even if very partially, higher realities that could satisfy them. "A man's physical hunger does not prove that man will get any bread; he may die of starvation on a raft in the Atlantic," Lewis writes. "But surely a man's hunger does prove that he comes of a race which repairs its body by eating and inhabits a world where eatable substances exist."[8] Our sense of distraction, discontentment, and dislocation—and the inhumane, exhausting effects those sensations have on our daily lives—should make us confident that there is, in fact, an alternative.

You may know Philippians 4:8 by heart:

> Finally, brothers, whatever is true, whatever is honorable, whatever is just, whatever is pure, whatever is lovely, whatever is commendable, if there is any excellence, if there is anything worthy of praise, think about these things.

Many of us memorized this verse as children or teens. We heard it taught often, and for good reason. Here is one of Scripture's clearest and most easily applicable teachings on guarding our minds. Paul lays it out simply: choose to think about that which is true, honorable, just, pure, lovely, commendable, excellent, and praiseworthy. Here we sense a possible way out of the minutiae of the digital age. Like a strainer that catches the foreign objects and allows the good broth to flow, these qualities could arrest our hearts and keep us from the despair of distraction, discontentment, and dislocation.

The passage right before this one is famous in its own right too, but most of the time, you see it separated from verse 8. Verses 6 and 7 read:

> Do not be anxious about anything, but in everything by prayer and supplication with thanksgiving let your requests be made known to God. And the peace of God, which surpasses

8   C. S. Lewis, *The Weight of Glory: And Other Addresses* (New York: HarperCollins, 1949), 32.

all understanding, will guard your hearts and your minds in Christ Jesus.

We should contemplate more seriously the possibility that the devotedness of our thought life is connected to the question of whether God's peace is conquering anxiety in our hearts. Rather than reading these as two totally separate commands—don't be anxious, trust God with your requests (vv. 6–7), and also guard your thought life (v. 8)—what if we read them as two sides of the same command? What if the foundation of a thought life that was characterized by truth, honor, purity, and excellence is a heart that has its anxieties quieted by the peace of God?

As we've surveyed the different ways the online age shapes us, we've consistently found that, insofar as they are dominated by the values and habits of the web, our minds are restless. We wander intellectually, outsourcing wisdom to whichever person or group we like or dislike. We wander spiritually, tirelessly shaping an identity as fragile as the glass screens we construct it with. We wander sexually, turning human intimacy into a consumable good. Our digital technology has imported its values of immediacy and fleetingness into our souls. This results in more amazing products and greater feelings of efficiency and control over our world but at the high cost of a suffocating sense of anxiety. The age of connection is the age of loneliness. The age of productivity is the age of burnout. Why? Because we are not at peace.

Yet we are not without a Savior who promised us peace. "Peace I leave with you; my peace I give to you" (John 14:27). The peace of Jesus does not look like the anxious assertion of control that we practice in our digital habitats. Rather, peace is when we take our attention off ourselves and look up. "In everything by prayer and supplication with thanksgiving let your requests be made known to God." Here we have a physical practice—prayer—that brings us out of ourselves enough to behold Christ, the goodness of his listening heart, and the promise that he hears those who belong to him.

In prayer, distraction gives way to attentiveness: instead of letting the fog of a thousand curiosities or boredoms or worries drive us into therapeutic digital overload, we say, "I need peace, and I need it from Jesus," and we go to him. God does not want our attention to spread butter thin. He revealed himself to us in Jesus precisely so we would know him, so that our restless search for meaning and identity and forgiveness would end in his presence.

In prayer, discontent gives way to assurance. Because of the gospel, we know that peace for our anxieties does not depend finally on us. There's no influencer status we must reach before the King of the universe will consider us worthy of his peace. Paul can assure the Philippians that the peace of God will come into them as they pray because it's a peace won for them by the one who made peace by his blood (Col. 1:20). When our digital habitats make our lives look small, Christ can make our destiny look glorious.

In prayer, dislocation gives way to presence. The Bible's promise is that as we make our requests known to God, his peace will not only become available but will guard our hearts and minds in Christ Jesus. Wherever we find ourselves in God's providence, we can know that his peace is guarding us in Christ Jesus because we ourselves are "in" Christ Jesus. "And because of him you are in Christ Jesus, who became to us wisdom from God, righteousness and sanctification and redemption" (1 Cor. 1:30). We don't have to constantly pine for the world on the other side of our screen. We don't have to be divided in two between attention and presence. Wherever we are, we are in Christ Jesus, so we can be all there.

Nothing about our present situation can threaten to undo us, so we can choose to turn our focus and our love on the people and places that are actually in our God-ordained path. In Christ, no matter where we are, we are always on our way home.

The thought life that feasts on the riches of the true, the just, and the lovely is the thought life that is radically liberated by the peace of God that overcomes our restless, screen-weary souls as we ask for it.

The beloved Christian counselor David Powlison once did a thought experiment that genuinely changed my life. Powlison, trying to help other Christians see what incredible life-giving promises they have in Jesus, penned what he called an "antispsalm," literally, a psalm written from the opposite perspective. Taking the words of Psalm 23, Powlison turned the psalm, line by line, into a passage that emphasizes how many people *feel* in their day-to-day lives. Instead of, "The LORD is my shepherd; I shall not want," Antipsalm 23 declares:

I'm on my own. No one looks out for me or protects me.
I experience a continual sense of need. Nothing's quite right.

Powlison remarks, "The antipsalm tells what life feels like and looks like whenever God vanishes from sight."[9] He's right. And the minutiae of the digital world can overwhelm us with the sensations in this antipsalm. We feel worthless compared to others. We feel stretched to our absolute max, with no way to keep up. We feel somewhere else entirely. But the peace of God that passes understanding brings us back. On our most digitally saturated day, what

9   David Powlison, "Sane Faith in the Insanity of Life, Part 1," Christian Counseling and Educational Foundation, https://www.ccef.org/.

we need is to stop long enough to cry out to our Creator to give us his peace, to take care of us where we are, to make our anxious hearts lie down in green pastures. We need the one who planned all the days of our lives to lead us beside still waters, to restore our souls, and to comfort us even in the shadow of death. We need something to feast on, something good and merciful to welcome us, and somewhere to dwell forever.

And that's exactly what God offers:

The LORD is my shepherd; I shall not want.
    He makes me lie down in green pastures.
He leads me beside still waters.
    He restores my soul.
He leads me in paths of righteousness
    for his name's sake.

Even though I walk through the valley of the shadow of death,
    I will fear no evil,
for you are with me;
    your rod and your staff,
    they comfort me.

You prepare a table before me
    in the presence of my enemies;
you anoint my head with oil;
    my cup overflows.
Surely goodness and mercy shall follow me
    all the days of my life,
and I shall dwell in the house of the LORD forever.

Conclusion

Habits of Wisdom and Resistance

THE PRECEDING EIGHT CHAPTERS of this book exist primarily to convince you of two truths. First, the Bible lays out the wisdom we need to live faithfully and fruitfully before our Creator. Second, the internet is an epistemological and moral habitat that makes such wisdom seem like foolishness. By digging deep into the effects of the web, we can see its shape more clearly. As we contrast our digital habitats with biblical wisdom, we see the way God's word reorients us and pulls us back from the beliefs and attitudes that we tend to cultivate online.

So what now? It's one thing to see how all this works. It's another to know what life should or can look like in light of it.

When it comes to the web and the Christian life, the question, "So what do I do now?" is especially tricky. Why? Because there's no straight line from Christian wisdom to rejection of technology. Simply because these digital liturgies are especially prevalent in online spaces doesn't mean they were created there. Rather, the dynamics we've looked at in this book exist because they were manufactured first in human hearts. Biblically, we must admit that, as Jesus said, "out of the abundance of the heart the mouth speaks" (Matt. 12:34). Even if you could throw away all your computers and smartphones, delete all your social media accounts, and go back to physical CDs and newspapers, your heart would still tilt away from the wisdom of Christ. Sin is holistic and fundamental, which means we can't be rid of it by taking any external actions.

But there's another reason that a blanket rejection of technology won't work. Put simply, there's no putting Pandora back in her box. The technological revolutions that gave us digital ways of life cannot and will not be reversed. Most Western economies now depend on vast amounts of connectivity, and many jobs simply require large amounts of time spent online. The world has been permanently transformed by this technology. Thus the challenge of cultivating Christian wisdom in a digital age will repeat itself every generation, through different hardware, different cultural moods, and different temptations along the way.

But even more importantly, the decisiveness of the digital revolution is a fact not just for us, but for our neighbors. Even if it were possible to order one's life in the twenty-first century to eschew all forms of the internet and digital communication, the end result would mostly just be to cut us off from other people, the majority of whom would continue to live, work, think, and consume online, with no sense of how their hearts and minds might be changing for the worse.

Finally, we need to remember that the digital age is not an exception to Scripture's promise that "no temptation has overtaken you that is not common to man" (1 Cor. 10:13). While the technologies that dominate our world are very new, the spiritual and human problems we encounter in them are not. Crafting an identity instead of receiving the one God has given us is as old as building a tower that reaches to heaven. Forfeiting the pursuit of truth in favor of picking and choosing what you will believe is what God's people have done in every idol we've ever constructed for ourselves, whether made of gold, money, or power. Paul told the Corinthians that love does not "rejoice at wrongdoing" (1 Cor. 13:6)—a command that would obliterate online shaming if we ever let it.

One of the best things about the Bible is that the deeper you look into it, the more it seems to speak very specifically to the world as it is right now. We moderns flatter ourselves when we speak of living in "unprecedented times." Scripture knows better. There is nothing new under the sun. Thus the quest to live wisely in a digital age is simply another expression of the same journey God's people have been on in every generation since Eden. We ought not be intimidated by novelty. God's word is evergreen: it never loses charge, it never requires an update, and it never leaves us feeling empty.

So with that said, let us consider what we need to navigate a world of these digital liturgies: specifically, the *practices*, the *people*, and the *promises* we need.

Practices

For most of my life, I have believed that the way meaningful transformation works is this:

1. I earnestly pray for and try to generate strong feelings.
2. Once these strong feelings are achieved, doing the right thing will feel natural.

As I've talked to people my age about the things we've learned about the Christian life as we've gotten older, one of the consistent themes in these conversations is the discovery—often well after adolescence—that this isn't how most change works. It's not what the Bible actually teaches, and it's not even really feasible. Scripture does have a lot to say about our feelings: "God loves a cheerful giver" (2 Cor. 9:7); "Love the Lord with all your heart and with all your soul and with all your mind" (Matt. 22:37); "Rejoice in the Lord always" (Phil. 4:4). These commands are indeed aimed at our emotions, and there's no question that when Christ raises a person from spiritual death to life, he creates radically new affections, not just new behavior.

But over the past few years, I have discovered in Scripture a theme that I had missed for a long time: the theme of habits. Habits are the DNA of Israel's year of worship in the Old Testament. God commands his people to make regular sacrifices and regular offerings; to regularly gather to hear his word and offer worship; and, most tellingly to me, to assemble at regular times and seasons for feasts and festivals that remind the nation about God's goodness and his works of redemption. When God commanded his people to love him with all their heart, he did not mean that they should sacrifice only when they *feel* guilty, make offerings only when they *feel* grateful, or hold a feast only when they *feel* blessed. Instead, what God gave his people was a set of practices, a regular rhythm of actions that could train their spirits and shape them more into holiness.

In our spiritual lives, we often seem to intuitively know the value of regular rhythms. That is why habits such as reading Scripture, prayer, and faithful membership in a local church are integral to growing as believers. But the importance of habits goes beyond the typical spiritual checklist items. Habits create habitats for our hearts; they shape our identity and train our desires so that our feelings, which can change quickly, are not solely bearing up the weight of our character.

In his bestselling book *Atomic Habits*, James Clear sums up how habits relate to our identity:

> Every habit is like a suggestion: "Hey, maybe *this* is who I am." If you finish a book, then perhaps you are the type of person who likes reading. If you go to the gym, then perhaps you are the type of person who likes exercise. . . . Every action you take is a vote for the type of person you wish to become. No single instance will transform your beliefs, but as the votes build up, so does the evidence of your new identity.[1]

This sounds a lot like the New Testament's theme of "becoming who you are."[2] Justification is the legal declaration that Christ has paid for our sins and accomplished a perfect record of righteousness on our behalf. Sanctification is the process by which we are transformed by the Spirit more into the image of Jesus. How do these two realities work together in the Christian life? I believe an important answer in Scripture is that, by the Spirit, we pursue habits that shape our character in the direction of our justified identity. Paul writes:

> If then you have been raised with Christ, seek the things that are above, where Christ is, seated at the right hand of God. Set your minds on things that are above, not on things that are on earth. For you have died, and your life is hidden with Christ in God. When Christ who is your life appears, then you also will appear with him in glory. (Col. 3:1–4)

1 James Clear, *Atomic Habits: An Easy and Proven Way to Build Good Habits and Break Bad Ones* (New York: Avery, 2018), 38.
2 The first person I heard use this phrase was John Piper.

"Seek the things that are above" and "set your minds on things that are above" are commands to practice habits. What kind of habits? Habits consistent with a person who is "hidden with Christ" and "raised with Christ." Identity and habits go together. It's not merely an issue of feeling strong enough about your identity in Christ to seek the things that are above. It's about seeking those things because that is where your life, in Christ, really is.

I've belabored this point, and there is still much that could be said about the role of habits in the Christian life. But for now, let us proceed as if we are convinced that habits matter. *What kind* of habits should we cultivate in the pursuit of Christian wisdom in a digital age?

Ask yourself some hard questions. When was the last time you read a book, listened to music, or had a conversation for more than an hour without checking your phone? When was the last time you sat alone with your thoughts with no email, no social media, and no streaming? I'm convinced many of us feel we don't know how to focus, simply for lack of practice. Every area of life is saturated with noise; we fidget in moments of stillness and silence, instinctively wanting our devices to rescue us from such unsettling inactivity. Thus, a habit of resistance might begin merely with one hour each day that we intentionally retreat from digital technology.

If you work in an information job that demands connectivity, consider taking a tech-free lunch hour, seeking out a book, a conversation, or a rewarding hobby instead of scrolling social media or catching up on the latest Netflix offering. Identify the specific channels through which the web seems to dominate your attention. Is it online news? Consider subscribing to a physical magazine or newspaper to cultivate the kind of deep reading that computers subvert. Is YouTube a default attention magnet? Instead of nibbling on clips all day, use a content blocker to restrict access during the day and look forward to watching an entire movie later. Whereas YouTube's bite-sized format is mostly distraction fodder, losing ourselves in a truly captivating story has a way of deeply moving and refreshing us.

Generally speaking, the more our attention is diffused over a thousand minute things—which is how our attention works when we're deeply plugged into the web—the more scrambled and exhausted we will be. There's no magic formula for resisting this. Again, this is not a book telling you to delete your accounts and throw away your devices. The key is to understand how digital technology affects us and to engage with it accordingly. For most of us, the biggest challenge is simply changing how we default. When there's nothing that immediately commands our attention, where do we give it? Changing the answer to that question is a fundamental part of deep resistance to the digital liturgies.

People

One of my favorite films is Robert Zemeckis's 2000 drama *Cast Away.* One of the most famous scenes from that movie depicts the marooned Chuck Noland (played by Tom Hanks) using a bloody hand to create "Wilson," a volleyball that becomes his only companion for four years on a deserted island. Completely alone and running low on hope that he will ever be rescued, Chuck gives Wilson a face and even some grass "hair," and begins to talk to Wilson as if he were a true human companion.[3]

In another kind of movie, this would be a gag, a joke meant to make us laugh at Chuck's silliness. But Zemeckis and writer

---

3   *Cast Away*, directed by Robert Zemeckis (Los Angeles: 20th Century Fox, 2000).

William Broyles Jr. portray this not as a joke but as something deeply profound about human nature. Chuck knows that Wilson is a volleyball. But he also knows that without some sense of embodied presence beside him on that island, he will quickly lose his mind. Wilson becomes just as important to Chuck's survival as the fire he learns to create and the fish he learns to hunt. Watching this, the audience is meant not to laugh at Chuck but to admit that we, too, would need some kind of "Wilson" to keep us from crushing despair in our loneliness.

Modern Western culture is profoundly lonely. This is true even despite the astonishing mobility and connectedness of our world. Never before has travel been easier, safer, or more affordable. Never before has instant communication with someone across the planet been so common. Yet a great number of people, particularly young adults, do not feel connected to anyone. We have discovered instead that our hypermobility has made us feel homeless, and our social networks have made us feel friendless. We've forgotten what Chuck Noland knew right away: embodied presence matters.

The fact is that near the center of many of our most significant advances in digital technology has been a profound dehumanization. By separating our personhood from technique, many modern devices express within themselves the logic of radical isolation. The GPS means that knowing a neighborhood is never mandatory. The backward-facing camera means we never need to ask someone else to take a picture. During the COVID-19 pandemic, billions of people around the world experienced a severe disruption to their lives through enforced isolation. But perhaps even more telling was how *un*disrupted so many parts of our lives were. For many of us, work transitioned smoothly to remote settings, as emails and video calls replaced coworkers. Churches began streaming their services, and for many people the "experience" of church on their TV or laptop hardly missed a beat from their "experience" of going to church.

We have become exceedingly good at replacing human beings with technology. But even as our performance at work and media intake have kept apace, our spirits have not. We need people. We need presence. We need place.

To actively resist the dehumanization of much digital technology, we have to do something simple yet often difficult: we must gather. And while there are many things we could say about cultivating interpersonal relationships, seeking the faces of others and not just their usernames, arguably the most important gathering we can seek out as Christians is the gathering of our local church. It is in this gathering that our Maker and Redeemer promises to be present himself. "For where two or three are gathered together in my name, there am I in the midst of them" (Matt. 18:20 KJV). It is this gathering where we not only recover part of what it means to be an embodied person, but we draw nearer together to becoming *fully* human, transformed into the image of the eternal Son of God, the most human person in history.

To resist the digital liturgies, we need regular immersion into the embodied community of God. We need to sing to one another, to exhort one another, to encourage one another, to forgive one another, and to laugh and cry with one another. The more we do so, the more transparent the facade of digital selfhood will become. We can't just mute or unfollow a fellow church member who irritates us. We must learn civil, sacrificial love. We can't fast-forward through a convicting message we are sitting in. We must allow the word to cut us open so it can put us back together again. Church is gospel givenness.

Again, there is much more we could say about recovering embodied presence. Sunday church is by no means the only legitimate way of gathering with others.[4] But I single out church for two reasons. First, as mentioned above, the local church is crucial for our spiritual lives. Second, the ascendance of "virtual church" means that many Christians are struggling with the motivation to be physically present at a service they very well could stream. But this struggle reflects both a misunderstanding of church and of the web. The church is not simply an exhibition of spirtual events for public spectacle, but a living institution where the Holy Spirit meets with his people, independent of how effectively we "downloaded" the sermon or the music into our mental memory.

But virtual church is also a misunderstanding of the web. As we've seen, form creates meaning. The web is not simply another way to do all the things we do offline. It's an entirely new epistemological and spiritual habitat. It shapes everything on it into its image. If, as I've argued, the wisdom of God is necessarily given and embodied, it is impossible to meaningfully be shaped by that wisdom in an exclusively digital context. When we physically gather, we learn what cannot be learned in other ways, and we are shaped in ways we cannot be shaped in other ways.

Promises

Finally, to resist the digital liturgies of our age, we need promises. If we're being honest, much of what I've said in this chapter might sound like spiritualized technique. "Do this, don't do that, and

---

4 For more about pursuing a life of embodied fellowship and love, I recommend Andy Crouch's book *The Life We're Looking For: Reclaiming Relationship in a Technological World* (New York: Convergent, 2022).

you will be a wise person." Advice is good. But what about the days when this quest for Christian wisdom feels hopeless? What about the times when the world's frenetic madness and insanity seem certain to overcome us? What about the moments when we are so screen-addled, so muddied in our thinking and empty in our identity and relationships, that everything in us just wants to scroll to keep the anxiety at bay?

The good news in these moments is that wisdom isn't just something we must attain. It is actually a person. Jesus Christ is not just wise. He is wisdom. Paul writes that we "are in Christ Jesus, who became to us wisdom from God, righteousness and sanctification and redemption" (1 Cor. 1:30). In the book of Proverbs, wisdom is personified as a virtuous woman who calls to the people, exhorting them to come learn from her. In one of Lady Wisdom's great speeches, she declares:

The LORD possessed me at the beginning of his work,
    the first of his acts of old.
Ages ago I was set up,
    at the first, before the beginning of the earth.
When there were no depths I was brought forth,
    when there were no springs abounding with water.
Before the mountains had been shaped,
    before the hills, I was brought forth,
before he had made the earth with its fields,
    or the first of the dust of the world.
When he established the heavens, I was there; . . .
    then I was beside him, like a master workman,
and I was daily his delight,
    rejoicing before him always,

rejoicing in his inhabited world
and delighting in the children of man. (Prov. 8:22–31)

This language leads many biblical scholars to believe that Lady Wisdom is a mysterious image of Jesus himself. Wisdom's preexistence along with God before the creation of the world reminds us of John 1, in which the divine Word (Christ) "was in the beginning with God" and "all things were made through him, and without him was not any thing made that was made" (John 1:2–3). To pursue wisdom is to pursue a person. In seeking wisdom we are seeking not an abstract set of ideas, not merely a collection of insights to make life go more smoothly. We are searching for Christ himself.

God's giving of himself to us in Christ is a life-changing promise. If wisdom were simply a thing, we could never be sure we would find it. Everything would rise or fall on how well we looked, how determined we were to find it, how deeply we were able to ingrain its lessons. In a world in which we found ourselves constantly slipping into unthinking cooperation with the spirit of the age, we would despair of ever being able to really hold onto wisdom, even if we ever found it.

But because wisdom is a person, we receive promises to fall back on. In Proverbs 9 we hear the patient invitation that wisdom gives those who need it:

Wisdom has built her house;
she has hewn her seven pillars.
She has slaughtered her beasts; she has mixed her wine;
she has also set her table.
She has sent out her young women to call
from the highest places in the town,

"Whoever is simple, let him turn in here!"
  To him who lacks sense she says,
"Come, eat of my bread
  and drink of the wine I have mixed.
Leave your simple ways, and live,
  and walk in the way of insight." (Prov. 9:1–6)

Wisdom presents a sumptuous feast, the kind that would really satisfy, warming and strengthening us from the inside out. It is not the already proficient that wisdom calls, but the "simple," the one who "lacks sense." Those who don't have are welcome to come and receive. This isn't just a one-time announcement. Wisdom is calling all over, "from the highest places in the town," actively pursuing those who don't deserve it.

This isn't just truthful thinking or clever living. This is grace.

We get a clearer picture of what wisdom's bread and wine really are in the Gospels. Jesus tells the people, "I am the bread of life; whoever comes to me shall not hunger, and whoever believes in me shall never thirst" (John 6:35). In offering bread and drink, Jesus (wisdom) offers himself. By dying in the place of fools, Jesus offers himself as wisdom incarnate to any who would come. This is why Paul could declare that Christ crucified is nothing less than the "power of God and the wisdom of God" (1 Cor. 1:24). Wisdom is realized in the embrace of Jesus Christ, who reveals God, ourselves, and our world perfectly to us. Our foolishness is absorbed by his blood, and we are free to learn from a gentle and lowly teacher (Matt. 11:29).

And we have his promise that as we trust in him, his Spirit empowers us to take every thought captive to him (2 Cor. 10:5). In a world of unceasing noise, his voice *will* break through and lead us. In a world of rootless identity crisis, he reminds us that we belong to him, that we are created by and for him, and that he will wipe every tear from our eyes as we finally see the one face we have longed to see (Rev. 21). In a world of shame, he tells us that our record of debt is canceled and that nothing can separate us from his love. In a world of lust, he offers his own broken body in the place of our defiled body (Luke 22:19). The digital liturgies that captivate so easily wither in light of who our wisdom really is and how much he has done, is doing, and will do for us.

Conclusion

The God of Scripture is a sovereign God. By his decree, our digital technologies have come to fruition. Nothing has surprised God or taken him off guard. He knows exactly the kind of challenges facing us today. In fact, they come, finally, from his all-controlling, all-wise, all-good will.

In our online technologies God has given us some wondrous gifts. We do well to enjoy them, praising him for his goodness in sharing them with us. But like the silver and gold that Israel took from Egypt in the Lord's miraculous conquest on their behalf, and shaped into a golden calf for worship, the material gifts that God gives can become idols. The digital liturgies that vie for our belief and our attention are simply man-made structures posing as real identity, real wisdom, real pleasure, and real justice. They entrance us because they know our hearts are restless for these things, and we cannot live for long without the hope of finding them.

The web is a curious, marvelous thing. But at the end of the day, I believe its power and its appeal are simple. The web is a promise that we can be more than we are, do more than we can, and feel more than is near us. The web lays its billions of pages out in front of us, its incalculable hours of "content," and beckons us to a place where there can be fullness of joy—a place we are freed from our dying bodies, liberated from the search for home, and emancipated to experience nothing but newness. In fact, I think that every time we log on, we are looking for something. We are looking for heaven. The pieces of the past that we preserve on social media? That's a search for heaven. The effort to stay so much "in the know" that we never feel threatened or uneasy about the state of the world? That's a search for heaven.

Someone who knew about our search for heaven was C. S. Lewis. In his sermon "The Weight of Glory," Lewis described our search for heaven as a "desire" that awakens in the most powerful moments of our life. We experience it enough to ache to find the place, the "country," where it all comes from. But what Lewis knew was that this ache for a beauty that would change us at the deepest level of our being is an ache only someone beyond us can truly satisfy:

> In speaking of this desire for our own far off country, which we find in ourselves even now, I feel a certain shyness. I am almost committing an indecency. I am trying to rip open the inconsolable secret in each one of you—the secret which hurts so much that you take your revenge on it by calling it names like Nostalgia and Romanticism and Adolescence; the secret also which pierces with such sweetness that when, in very intimate conversation, the mention of it becomes imminent, we grow awkward and affect to laugh at ourselves; the secret we cannot hide and cannot tell, though we desire to do both. We cannot tell it because it is a desire for something that has never actually appeared in our experience. . . .

The books or the music in which we thought the beauty was located will betray us if we trust to them; it was not in them, it only came through them, and what came through them was longing. These things—the beauty, the memory of our own past—are good images of what we really desire; but if they are mistaken for the thing itself they turn into dumb idols, breaking the hearts of their worshipers. For they are not the thing itself; they are only the scent of a flower we have not found, the echo of a tune we have not heard, news from a country we have never yet visited.[5]

But we *will* get there. And in the meantime, the person from whom all this beauty comes promises to open up his world and his word to us. We can be at peace. He is for us and with us.

---

5   C. S. Lewis, *The Weight of Glory: And Other Addresses* (New York: HarperCollins, 1949), 29–31.

Acknowledgments

THIS BOOK EXISTS because of many people. It has been one of the supreme humbling experiences of my life to be on the receiving end of so much love, help, wisdom, and counsel. I cannot possibly pay back what others have given me. I can only say with the psalmist that the lines have fallen for me in pleasant places.

First, I want to thank Crossway, especially Justin Taylor and Todd Augustine, for their encouragement and friendship. My friend Lydia Brownback was instrumental in encouraging me to take on this project.

The ideas in this book have emerged from many books, articles, and conversations. I want to thank Matt Smethurst for his mentorship and friendship. Collin Hansen, Ivan Mesa, Jake Meador, and Tim Challies have played enormous roles in my professional and intellectual life, and I am deeply indebted for their help and support. Karen Swallow Prior read this manuscript in record time and offered feedback that was transformative.

I owe profound gratitude to Nicholas Carr, whose book *The Shallows* I finished on a late summer evening on my in-laws' patio, and knew immediately that his work was going to mean something significant in my own life.

This manuscript wouldn't exist without the practical hospitality of many people who offered lodging, writing weekends, and service. Joe and Judy McHugh welcomed me into their beautiful home, and some of the best moments of writing happened there. Jordan Woodie and the people of Coral Hill Baptist Church graciously provided a getaway that proved to be crucial. This kindness is more than I can repay with words.

Finally, to my family. My in-laws Chuck and Kim Potts are the best "Mimi and Pop-Pop" anyone could ask for. I am grateful every day for you. My brothers-in-law Sam Emadi and Dan Maketansky are constant sources of strength and grace, and my sisters Corrie Ann and Rebecca were my first friends in this world, and still two of my best. Mom and Dad have made sacrifices incalculable, but more than anything else have surrounded my life (and this book) with prayers. I know Jesus Christ because of them.

Charlie, Ruthie, and Wesley: you are my pride and joy. Thank you for putting up with my absent weekends and extra-long nights, but most of all, thank you for being the three most beautiful gifts I've ever received.

My beloved Emily: you are the one my heart is tied to until eternity. Thank you for your help, your sacrifices, your inexhaustible words of love and encouragement. "What would I do without you?"

Study Questions

Introduction: What the Web Means for Our Spiritual Lives

1. What does the illustration about the fish and the water suggest about culture's effect on us all?

2. Is it accurate to describe the web as a "neutral tool"? Why or why not?

3. Is it possible to be shaped by something even without realizing it? What are some examples of this?

4. How do the things we consume tell us a story? What kind of stories do your favorite films, music, and social media apps tell you?

5. What is one example of a biblical truth that feels less plausible to you while you are immersed in social media or the web?

Chapter 1: Embodied Wisdom in a Faceless Age

1. How would you describe the difference between wisdom and knowledge?

2. Why does it matter that God created human beings with bodies? What does this fact tell us about the kind of world we live in?

3. Have you previously thought about your body as a crucial part of your identity? Why might thinking this way be difficult for some?

4. Why can people who are "connected" to hundreds of other people online still feel isolated and lonely?

5. What evidence can you see in the world today that people have a "computerlike" attitude toward reality?

Chapter 2: How Technology Shapes Us

1. Marshall McLuhan said, "The medium is the message." Do you agree? If so, what are some examples of media communicating messages? If you don't agree, why don't you?

2. The chapter gives a couple of examples of technologies that shape attitudes simply by virtue of what they do. Can you give a few other examples?

3. What is one reason that many modern Christians have not thought closely about technology's power to shape our spiritual lives?

4. What features of certain digital technologies might reflect the transhumanist convictions of their creators?

5. Do the stories of Dean and Erica hit close to home for you? What do you think someone like Dean or Erica needs to realize?

Chapter 3: Drowning in the Shallows

1. Can you think of any examples of how the influence of digital technology has made a difference in how you read, meditate, or relate to others?

2. How does the idea of neuroplasticity fit with the teaching of Scripture? Are there particular Bible passages or doctrines that support the notion that our brains actually change over time in response to stimuli?

3. What are some examples of "liturgies" in secular culture? How do these habits and environments affect how we feel?

4. This chapter states, "The web has revolutionized nearly every aspect of our lives." What are some practical examples of this revolution? What might a person who lived in the first half of the twentieth century make of our habits today?

5. How might the ideas in this chapter help you communicate more effectively with people around you?

Chapter 4: "My Story, My Truth"

1. What does it mean to say that the internet has "democratized" modern life? What are the benefits of this democratization? What are the drawbacks?

2. What is it about the nature of the internet that makes traditional, established sources of knowledge seem obsolete or even oppressive?

3. From a Christian perspective, what is good about an emphasis on authenticity? What is troubling?

4. When people's personal stories conflict with one another, how is this conflict usually resolved? What might this conflict tell us about the need for objective standards of truth?

5. What difference does having a Christian idea of personal identity make in everyday life?

Chapter 5: The Abolition of Thought

1. Can you recall watching an angry exchange online? What were some of the impressions you came away with?

2. How is the social internet designed to elicit our outrage?

3. What did Screwtape mean by "jargon"? What are some examples you've seen of jargon's effect on clear thinking?

4. Of the three characteristics of Christian thought, which do you think is most difficult to achieve?

5. How does believing the gospel make a difference in our feelings toward those who disagree with us?

Chapter 6: Shame on You

1. Have you ever experienced or known someone who experienced online shaming? If so, what was something that was surprising about it?
2. Explain how society can become both highly permissive ("you do you") and highly shaming.
3. What is it about social media that makes it a natural place for people to publicly shame and be shamed? What is an example of a social shaming that would probably not happen in a physical setting but could easily happen online?
4. How does the gospel deal with shame? How should believing the gospel transform our response to people who have transgressed moral or social norms in some way?

Chapter 7: Naked in the Dark

1. James writes, "Pornography is arguably the web's chief export." If this is true, what might be some effects of porn?
2. If the web is pornographically shaped, do you believe it is intrinsically evil? Why or why not?
3. Can you think of a time in your life when mere consumption replaced genuine living?
4. What are some practical dangers of the internet's power to deliver endless novelty?
5. How does the beauty of God's created world help us resist patterns of consumption?

Chapter 8: Death by Minutiae

1. Between distraction, discontentment, and dislocation, which do you find most tempting?
2. What sites or activities do you find most distracting online?
3. How might the technology of the "infinite scroll" make us numb spiritually?
4. What is Christian wisdom's answer to the modern problems of discontentment and dislocation?

Conclusion: Habits of Wisdom and Resistance

1. Should Christians totally reject the web? If so, why? If not, why not?
2. Given the omnipresence of the smartphone, what particular habits seem most important for navigating the digital age wisely?
3. How would you counsel someone who feels he or she needs constant online connectivity?
4. How can we be sure that Christ will make us wise?

General Index

heavenly citizenship, 104
hidden with Christ, 172
humility, 110, 146
hyperlinks, 59, 60
hypocrisy, 125

identity: created on social media, 29;
    and habits, 172; as received, 160
identity crisis, 180
image of God, 16, 24, 26–27, 29, 119
imitation of Christ, 55
immanent frame, 118
impatience, 157
Inception (film), 33–34, 48
in Christ, 164–65
individualism, 139
Industrial Revolution, 38
"infinite scroll," 135
Inner Ring, 106–7
inner self, and physical self, 28
Instagram, 157–58
intellectual technologies, 53
intellectual wandering, 163
internet: as bidirectional, 58; centered
    on the self, 79; changing the
    brain, 51; consciousness-bending
    format, 60–61; creates new pat-
    terns of belief and behavior, 66; as
    epistemological habitat, 9, 57–61,
    66, 99, 167, 176; formative power
    of, 9, 13, 79; form undermines
    reconciliation, 10; as foundational
    medium, 62; growth in use of, 7;
    moral language of, 63; narrative
    of, 65–66; as "opt-in" medium,
    66; as "opt-out" medium, 66; and
    pornography, 8, 134, 139–42; as
    radically egalitarian, 72; as "uni-
    versal medium," 51
internet porn. *See* pornography
inventor, ideology of, 44
isolation, 19, 31, 138–39, 174

Jacobs, Alan, 125
jargon, 98–99

Jesus: death on the cross, 88; as wisdom
    from God, 177–80
Jobs, Steve, 42
judgment, 123, 126
justification, 171

Kenyon College, 3–4, 11
kindness, 146
Kleinig, John, 27, 159–60
knowledge of good and evil, 28
Kubrick, Stanley, 18, 20
Kurzweil, Ray, 42

Lewis, C. S., 98, 102, 106–7, 161,
    181–82
lifestyle influencers, 158
likes, not a measure of truth, 108
limitless freedom, 86
loneliness, 19, 31, 163, 174
lone-rangerism, 108
Longman, Tremper, III, 20–23
"look in" approach to life, 6
love, 88, 145
Lukianoff, Greg, 71–72, 117
lust, 135–36, 139, 144, 180
Lyu, S. M., 22n5

McClay, Wilfred, 119–21
McLuhan, Marshall, 35–36, 51
material/immaterial dualism, 54
meaning, 95
meaninglessness, 118, 150
meditation, 153
"medium is the message," 51
meekness, 146
metaverse, 43
#MeToo, 82, 143
"middle way," 102
mind, renewal of, 110
"mindless refresh," 135
minutiae, 154–56
misinformation, 101
moral hypocrisy, 116
morality, has not disappeared, 122
Musk, Elon, 43
"my truth," 71, 75, 77, 79, 84

Whole Earth Catalog, 40–41
Wikipedia, 135
Winfrey, Oprah, 77
Winner, Langdon, 53
wisdom, 16, 20–26, 167; difficult and
    unappealing on the internet, 99;
    in digital age, 168; as holistic,
    20; seems like foolishness, 167;

as submission to God's good and
    given reality, 31
wisdom literature, 21
World Wide Web. *See* internet

YouTube, 2, 135, 137

Zemeckis, Robert, 173
Zuckerberg, Mark, 43

Scripture Index